D0810660

"From the very first page of the introduction, this wonderful book gripped me by the heart. It awakened me to life's mysterious, intoxicating beauty. Buck is a masterful painter with words. Each portrait here is a rich reminder that our journey is caressed by the unmistakable fingertips of God. What a treasure! Thank you, Buck!"

—**Randy Stonehill**, international CCM recording artist,
Christian Music Hall of Fame member

"What a fun read! Buck Storm takes you on an intriguing Holy Land journey as he moves though all corners of Israel—Mount Hermon in the north, Eilat in the south, En Gedi in the east, Tel Aviv in the west, and iconic Jerusalem in the middle. His descriptions and observations of Israeli people intertwined with his personal stories of his travels in the land—while tying everything into God's Word—makes this an extraordinary page-turner!"

—**Bill Perkins**, founder and executive director,
Compass International

"With the heart of a songwriter and the eye of a poet, Buck Storm is unquestionably one of today's master storytellers. I have never been to Israel, but he has managed—through these beautiful and insightful essays—to bring the best of Israel to me. Here is a book not just to be read, but to be read again and again."

—**Ann Tatlock**, novelist, editor, and children's book author

"There are many books one can read that are 'about' Israel, with analysis, history, dates, and facts. Buck Storm's anecdotes bring readers 'to' Israel and introduce them to real people—individuals living in Israel with their own stories. Whether you are considering traveling to Israel yourself and want to know what you might experience, or you just want to see beyond the geopolitical analysis and be transported to Israel through words, I highly recommend this book. You'll laugh, learn, and be moved by the narrative."

—**Glen Iverson**, Holy Ground Explorations

"I know Buck Storm well. I've had the pleasure of regularly accompanying him in various music endeavors since the turn of the century, and I've been to Israel numerous times with some of the people he mentions in this book. As I read *Finding Jesus in Israel*, I can hear Buck's voice as if he's sitting right next to me—both of us on the back porch, feet up with a hot cup of coffee in hand. I hope that you'll enjoy getting to know Buck, his unique voice, and his incredible perspective on Israel and her people. He has a rare gift for discovering the sacred in almost every situation, no matter how extraordinary or mundane."

—**Tod Hornby**, associate pastor,
Lake City Church, Coeur d'Alene, ID

"Buck Storm draws you in right from the introduction. He brings Israel up close and personal and makes you feel like you were there with him even if you have never been! The beauty, landscape, and traditions of the land are all beautifully woven together with Buck, the people, and Jesus. The personal stories bring Israel to life. His love for this small country— with all of its history, troubles, misunderstanding, and biblical truths— is evident. And when you are done reading, you will love the place too."

—**Pastor Mike Evers**, Island Christian Fellowship

"Buck Storm has an intriguing style of writing—you feel as if you are on the journey with him. I've been to Israel fifteen times, each time with a tour guide. Buck's detail to the ordinary floods my mind with those images while his knowledge of the land's culture and history is impressive. You will enjoy traveling with Buck through the Holy Land, and it only costs the price of a book!"

—**Pastor Bill Stonebraker**, Calvary Chapel of Honolulu

"Buck Storm's colorful personality, unique stories, and obvious love for the Lord Jesus Christ and Israel will make *Finding Jesus in Israel* a delight for any reader. This book will especially be insightful to those who seek to honor Scripture by 'praying for the peace of Jerusalem.' May God bless all those who read this book with a closer walk with Him!"

—**Dr. Tim Pollock**, The Home Church, Lodi, CA

"Buck Storm is a wonderful writer in both tune and tome. Mixed with a heart for God and a love for people, his writing is both encouraging and purposeful."

—**Pastor Ben Ortize**, Grace Sandpoint church, Sandpoint, ID

"Sometimes I feel sorry for those folks who visit Israel in the multiple big-bus tours or those who zoom in and out from cruise ships, because I know they will never experience the Israel that Buck Storm writes about. I love Buck's stories and his quirky writing style (kind of reminds me of Anne Lamott). Make sure a trip to the 'land where it all began' is on your short list, and I pray that you, too, can have your own stories to tell!"

—**Dr. Dan Stolebarger**, Holy Ground Explorations

"This is not just information on a page about a special place; it is a wellspring of inspiration. Prepare to have your faith stirred in a most delightful way!"

—**Pastor Robert Case**, Calvary Chapel Eastside, Bellevue, WA

"I've visited the Holy Land six times, and every time it's a once-in-a-lifetime experience. There's always something new—something out of the blue—that makes me want to go again. *Finding Jesus in Israel* is so descriptive in bringing the land and the people alive, I felt as though I was on a personal tour with Buck Storm as the guide. After reading his book, I'm ready to go again right now."

—**Richie Furay**, Rock & Roll Hall of Fame inductee,
founding member of Buffalo Springfield, Poco,
and Souther-Hillman-Furay bands,
founding pastor of Calvary Chapel, Broomfield, CO

"I love reading Buck Storm's novels because his story lines and character development are so wonderfully amazing. In reading *Finding Jesus in Israel*, a travelogue/memoir of Buck's real-life adventures in Israel, the story line and character development are even more wonderful, because they are based on real-life people, places, and encounters."

—**Pastor Danny Perry**, Calvary Chapel, Raymond, WA

"From the Golan to Eilat, Buck Storm will traverse 'the land' and march around your heart blowing his witty storytelling trumpet until the walls come tumbling down from the joy of confirming your own reservations to trek around God's aorta on earth. As a veteran of dozens of trips and producer of several records in Jerusalem, I could smell the *Za'atar* spices coming off the pages. *Finding Jesus in Israel* is a must-read for those who have trekked the Holy Land and an appetizer for those who have pondered."

—Paul Clark, singer, songwriter, recording artist, producer, photographer, author, craftsman, world traveler, follower of Jesus Christ, and friend to many

"With delightful whimsy, humor, and insertions of divine insight, Buck Storm takes us off the beaten path to explore places in the Holy Land that we would never dare to go—or even think of going. Not only did I find myself chuckling all the way through, but I discovered a strong hankering to reach for my boots and join him on the back roads."

—Rick Bundschuh, pastor of Kauai Christian Fellowship and author of *Soul Surfer* and other works

Finding Jesus in Israel

Through the Holy Land on the
ROAD LESS TRAVELED

Finding Jesus in Israel

Buck Storm

WORTHY®
PUBLISHING

Library of Congress Cataloging-in-Publication Data

Names: Storm, Buck, author.
Title: Finding Jesus in Israel : through the Holy Land on the road less traveled / Buck Storm.
Description: Franklin, TN : Worthy Publishing, 2018.
Identifiers: LCCN 2017060742 | ISBN 9781683971405 (hardcover)
Subjects: LCSH: Christian pilgrims and pilgrimages—Palestine. | Christian pilgrims and pilgrimages—Israel. | Palestine—Description and travel. | Israel—Description and travel.
Classification: LCC BV5067 .S76 2018 | DDC 263/.0425694—dc23
LC record available at https://lccn.loc.gov/2017060742

For foreign and subsidiary rights, contact rights@worthypublishing.com.

Published in association with Jim Hart of Hartline Literary Agency.

ISBN: 9781683971405

Cover Design: Kent Jensen | Knail
Cover Image: Dimitris Ouzounis, freeimages.com
Interior Design and Typesetting: Bart Dawson

Printed in the United States of America

18 19 20 21 22 23 LBM 8 7 6 5 4 3 2 1

IN LOVING MEMORY OF

WILBUR CLARENCE STORM

GIANT KILLER

Contents

Israel: A Crossroads

This place is a crossroads. Nowhere else does David's harp hold down the root chords to Robert Johnson's blues. This place wrecks you and uplifts you, breaks you and inspires you. It leaves you no wiggle room. It demands your attention.

When I was first approached with the idea of writing a book about my travels to Israel, I nodded politely, dropped it on the floor, and gave it a firm kick under the rug. I didn't mean to be rude, but while I love history, I'm no historian. I love the Bible, but I'm not a world-class theologian. I look forward to Christ's imminent return, but I'm certainly no eschatological genius. I know several who are all of the above. I've worked and traveled with them. We've broken bread together. I respect them. But I don't pretend to be one of them.

What I am is a songwriter. I'm a novelist with a couple of books under my belt. I'm a traveling troubadour and an observer of people. . . . I'm a storyteller. And truth be told, that's why—when no one was watching—I pulled the idea out from under the rug, wiped the dust off of it, and turned it over in my hands a few times.

You see, Israel draws me.

Just when I think I'm done with the place, off I go again, winging halfway around the world. The smells, the tastes, the sights, the feel of the air. . . . It's a land of extremes and a place of incredible dichotomy—exactly the stuff of which great stories are made. It's the land of patriarchs and prophets. Of Jacob, Job, and Jesus. Of wars and rumors of wars. Of Jezebel's dogs and jets kicking dust up off the Negev as they scream below sea level. It's David and Bathsheba, and legal prostitution advertised on the tart cards beneath the sturdy walking shoes of tourists rushing for buses that will take them to the Garden Tomb.

This land and its people have always played a part in my life.

I grew up with Bible stories. Sunday school in the church basement offered the flannelgraph kid version, but the real impact for me came during evenings listening to my grandpa pull tales from his old King James. The stories he told weren't about pairs of cartoon giraffes and elephants or a mellow, surfer Jesus with feathered hair. No, this was darker stuff. Battles and blood and sex and fire from heaven. Angels and devils in a great wrestling match over mankind. Here were kings and strongmen. Lion killers, prostitutes, heroes, and liars. If it had been a drive-in theater, my mom would have shoved my head down behind the back seat and told me to stay there. No, my grandpa's Bible wasn't rated PG-13, but in his living room I heard it unfiltered. I heard about men and women flawed to the core but loved wildly by their Creator and used for His glory.

I also heard about a shifty con man named Jacob, whose name God changed to Israel.

Israel . . .

Years later my grandpa finally made it to that land where so many of the stories he told took place. He returned with stories of his own, new friends, and five smooth stones from David's brook.

To me, my grandpa was a giant killer.

When he passed, I was asked if there was anything of his I'd like to have. Without hesitation I asked for that old King James Bible.

A decade or so later, my wife and I were invited on a Holy Land tour. Off we went on our first trip to Israel, me with guitar in hand and neither of us really knowing what to expect. I was so grateful to be invited to walk through the settings of the very stories I'd heard and read all my life. Caesarea, Jerusalem, the Garden of Gethsemane, the Sea of Galilee—these places impacted me deeply. I could have left Israel satisfied and gone back to my own journey, my own tales.

But then I had a moment.

It was a very cold and wet afternoon in the Golan Heights. A soldier stood beneath the darkening sky talking to our group about an October night in 1973. It was Yom Kippur—for Jews, the holiest day of the year—and Israel was under attack. They faced overwhelming odds, an Arab coalition led by Syria to the north and Egypt to the south. The word went out for all hands on deck, and our soldier was called out of bed to fight. I listened that day in the Golan as he spoke with deep emotion of friends and brothers who gave their lives in the hills above to protect the land of both their ancestors and their children.

As his story pulled me in deeper, the sky thundered and began to rain. All around me, people grumbled, broke away from the group, and headed back to the dry warmth of the bus. The soldier still talked, but only a couple of us remained. I saw tears in his eyes. And somehow, in that moment, I knew without a doubt I would return to this place.

It hit me hard: the story of Israel—the *real* story—isn't found in books. And not even in the comfortable baritone of my grandfather's voice. Israel's real story is written in the hearts and lives of her people. It is the unspoken tale behind a tired soldier's eyes. It tells of a journey that grinds on—haunted, hard, and beautiful. Here was Israel. Here was *Love*.

Israel is beautiful. Israel is vibrant. But Israel isn't clean. Far from it. Israel is sin, redemption, passion, and blood. At its heart, it's *human* and filled to the brim with the *world*—people of every religious, social, and political bent. The very ones God loved so much that He sent His Son to die for. Israel is a Palestinian kid on a roof in the old city beneath stars that dance like angels. It's the Jewish vendor in The Shuk—Jerusalem's huge outdoor market—cigarette dangling from the corner of his mouth, yelling and haggling with a housewife over the price of a fish. The guy in front of a desert gas station flirting with the female tourists and hawking rides on his sleepy-eyed camel. Pilgrims soaked in vibrating ecstasy on Easter morning as they march the *Via Dolorosa*, the path Jesus walked on His way to the cross.

At its very foundation, Israel is the story of God's interaction with mankind.

Me? I'm a self-admitted lousy tourist. The "back on the bus please exit through the gift shop" stuff definitely isn't my thing. So a few years ago my wife, Michelle, and I decided to start taking a few friends at a time, rent a van, and see Israel off the well-worn tourist trails. In the pages ahead, I don't promise facts and figures. I won't even swear to absolute accuracy. But you will see an amazing place, meet incredible people, and experience a living, ongoing story told to the best of my recollection, from the perspective of me—my grandpa's grandson.

CHAPTER 1

Please Exit through the Gift Shop

Think what you will about the Old Testament prophets, but Zechariah nailed it 2,500 years ago when he predicted Israel would one day be a thorn in the world's side. It's hard to imagine a country that could take a bath in Lake Michigan being a constant in news headlines. And yet it is. Israel is nothing if not polarizing.

Over three million people visit this little chunk of geography every year, most of them joining tours specifically tailored to their particular worldview. Bus routes crisscross: these careful bubbles of contained culture pass each other on the road. Jewish tours enjoy the modern mayhem of the beach cities, and they visit Masada, the Jerusalem synagogues, the Western Wall, and Yad Vashem—the Holocaust Center with its museum and memorial. Catholics track the shrine-topped sites deemed historical by Constantine's mother on her pilgrimage to trace the steps of Christ. Protestants and evangelicals ride tour boats on the Sea of Galilee and sing songs at the Garden Tomb. When sites are important to more than one group, people generally stick to their bubbles, astronauts on a space walk gathered around the tour guide's flag as if it is a lifeline to the mother ship.

Now don't get me wrong! These tours are amazing, even life changing. Israeli tour guides are without a doubt the best in the world, highly educated and truly passionate about the land and its history. Still, how do you see a whole country, even a small one, in just a week or two? How do you get a feel for the people—for their struggles, dreams, and passions? So much of Israel is bypassed simply because of time limitations, the number of tourists, and even (sometimes *especially*) the particular lens of your worldview glasses.

And with those glasses on, we can miss a lot of pearls while we rush to pick up stones.

One particular pearl, hidden for the most part from tourists and locals alike, is the Ramparts Walk, which is exactly what it sounds like: a trek that takes you around the narrow rampart of nearly all of Jerusalem's Old City wall. Just inside the Jaffa Gate you can duck into the information office, grab a ticket, climb some narrow stairs, and there you are, standing on top of parapets rebuilt by Suleiman the Magnificent, a sultan during the Ottoman Empire in the mid-sixteenth century. The bullet holes that pock the walls are reminders of the generations of soldiers who've guarded this place. This is a path of ghosts, my friends, and it's well traveled.

Old Jerusalem itself is divided into four general sections—Jewish, Christian, Muslim, and Armenian. Depending on which entrance you choose, you either head south past the Armenian and Jewish Quarters toward the Zion and Dung Gates, or you go north past the Christian and Muslim Quarters. Either way is fascinating. Birds flit in and out of the wall. The air smells of sunbaked stone, diesel fumes, and baking bread. On the street below, a busker sings a Dylan song in broken English. With this interplay of the old and the new, time seems to both roll by and blend into itself, giving you the impression you're part of something bigger. The thing I love best about this land is . . . you can't help being pulled out of *you.*

God spread a warm blanket of deep blue over Jerusalem on the day when a few friends and I took the northern route of the Ramparts Walk. I looked out across the Old City at the red-tiled rooftops of the Christian Quarter and, beyond them, at the domes and spires of the three religions that consider Jerusalem holy. The energy of the city was palpable. On a patio below, a woman lounged on a deck chair, reminding me of Bathsheba waiting for David to show. On my left, as I looked through a narrow slit in the wall, I saw modern Jerusalem sprawled over the hills, the city's white Jerusalem stone shining in the afternoon. A grassy park butted the wall below, and a man raced by on a beautiful, white Arabian mare. Where they came from I have no idea.

We passed the Latin Patriarchate, the Vatican's official presence in Israel, and then over the New Gate that connects the Old City's Christian Quarter with more modern West Jerusalem. The bells above the Church of the Holy Sepulchre pealed, competing with the voices of street vendors and traffic noise. Below us, courtyards resting in the shade offered a unique glimpse into the private lives of the people who call this place home. Farther on, steep steps climbed up and over the Damascus Gate. It was here a couple thousand years ago the apostle Paul began a journey that would change not only his life but the course of world history. The Damascus Gate edges the Muslim Quarter. This is obvious because of the altitude you gain hiking the Ramparts Walk. As I moved on, low domes began to top the buildings. I imagine there are very few places left on the planet devoid of those cosmos-beam-sucking and seemingly ever-present satellite dishes.

The aroma of spices delighted us, and we heard raised voices haggle in the market. Armed Israel Defense Forces (IDF) soldiers patrolled the streets, assault rifles at the ready. A large group of them gathered in front of Herod's Gate. I didn't stop to see what the ruckus was about. Sometimes in life—and sometimes in Israel—it's better to keep moving.

As we moved past a playground where the narrow walkway widened a bit, three young Palestinian boys laughed and shadow-boxed each other. I'd guess them to have been somewhere around nine or ten. As I approached, one of them flagged me with an outstretched palm. This guy was clearly the mouthpiece of the three. I took in his hole-riddled pants, worn sandals, and SpongeBob SquarePants t-shirt.

"Where did you come from?" he demanded in pretty passable English.

I motioned behind me. "Ramparts Walk. You a guard or something? Checking tickets?"

"What tickets? . . . I mean, where? USA?"

"Yeah. I'm from the USA."

He moved his hand to his forehead to block the sun. He and SpongeBob peered up at me simultaneously. "New York?"

"Everyone asks that. You know there are other parts of the US besides New York?"

"Yeah, I know. Cali?" he asked.

I laughed. "Nope, not California. I'm from Idaho. You know where that is?"

He looked me up and down like this was a stupid question. "Yeah. Iowa. Are you a cowboy?"

"Sometimes." I figured a little John Wayne street cred couldn't hurt.

As he considered what I'd said, I could practically hear the wheels turning in this little guy's head. He turned and pointed to his *compadres*. One of them held a skateboard that had seen better days. "You wanna see them ride that?"

I shrugged. After all, I was a guest here. "Why not? Where're they gonna ride it?"

He pointed to a narrow wall slanting at a steep angle toward the street.

I shook my head. No way. "Are you saying they're gonna ride down that? They *can* ride down that?"

"You wanna see?"

I have to admit I was curious at this point. "And not die?"

He nodded, eyes serious. "Yeah, they're cowboys."

I could smell the con, but I couldn't help liking the kid. "What's the catch, Tony Hawk?"

"Who is Tony Hawk? A cowboy?"

"Kind of. What's the catch?"

"What catch?"

"I mean, why are they gonna do it?"

"No catch, Iowa. They're cowboys."

"Idaho."

"Okay. You ready?"

"Are you gonna ask me for money?" Stupid question. Of course he was.

"You ready?" Good dodge. Clearly not this buckaroo's first rodeo.

"I was born ready."

The boy gave the signal.

I'm still not sure how they did it. I *am* sure several laws of physics were broken. But, no joke, both those guys managed to squeeze onto that one skateboard at the same time, and off they went. They screamed all the way down that crazy narrow ramp and landed in a raspberried but laughing heap on the asphalt at the bottom.

"What do you think?" SpongeBob said.

"I think that was 100 percent crazy, *amigo*. Do you ride down that too?"

In answer he held out his hand, palm up. "Give me the money, Iowa."

"I knew it," I said.

"American dollars."

"American dollars? Who are you? Al Capone?"

"Yeah. Al Capone. American dollars."

"You take shekels?"

He grinned when I dropped a few in his palm. The Evel Knievel twins were back at the top now.

"You wanna see me do it now?" SpongeBob said.

"I'm out of shekels."

He shrugged and turned his back to me.

Go back to Iowa, sucker.

I passed on. A few minutes later I heard more screaming behind me, then laughing as the board hit the bottom of the ramp. Maybe the new mark was from Idaho like me. Or maybe Cali.

Such is Jerusalem. It's a hardscrabble place, a lot of pain for a little gain. You watch your back, and you do what you have to do. Like anywhere else—whether Singapore, Cairo, New York, or even Iowa—people need an angle to survive.

A couple thousand years ago, just a few blocks away from where the SpongeBob gang worked the pilgrims, Jesus cried out, "O Jerusalem, Jerusalem, the one who kills the prophets and stones those who are sent to her! How often I wanted to gather your children together, as a hen gathers her chicks under her wings, but you were not willing!" (Matthew 23:37). The joint hasn't changed, but neither has He. Blood and history flow ankle-deep here, but love runs even deeper.

CHAPTER 2

Kerouac, Starlight, and a Curly Haired Dog

After a long day the sun sinks into the Negev on tired wings. Nothing comes easy in the desert. . . .

The beach city of Eilat hangs on the very southern tip of Israel like a drop of dew about to fall into the Red Sea. Egypt stretches to the west and Jordan to the east. South, across the water, the mountains of Saudi Arabia loom. The town itself is a modern place, but like everything in this part of the world, its foundations rest on hard-packed layers of history. Moses wandered here, for instance. In the Timna Valley just a few miles to the north, King Solomon mined for copper. The Queen of Sheba traveled through this area on her biblical journey to Jerusalem.

With access to both the Red Sea and the major trade routes of old, Egyptians, Nebateans, Romans, and others all have deep history here. Eilat is also Israel's jumping-off point for visiting the mind-boggling ruins of Petra across the border in Jordan. The small group I was with booked themselves a tour to do just that, and I drove them down, planning a couple of stops along the way to see some other ruins.

It's only a one-hour flight to Eilat from Jerusalem or Tel Aviv, but by car it's a long, hot grind through the desert. We left Jerusalem early and headed south. The day shone clear and beautiful. Have you ever seen the desert? Well, my friend, *that* is desert. A hard, lifeless place. We drove hours of empty highway. Once we saw a young Bedouin boy herding goats on a hillside. Miles later, a couple of Israeli tanks out on some military exercise kicked up a tall pillar of dust. An hour after that we passed two men on camels. One waved; the other never even looked our way.

The highway rolled on.

City lights shone along the Red Sea waterfront, and the sun died completely as we—hot, hungry, and roadweary—finally pulled into Eilat. I'd booked our overnight at the Sunset Motel, a place that sounded more like Route 66 than Israel. I'd never been there, but after circling several blocks—GPS can be dicey—we finally found it. A concrete and plaster wall with a heavy wooden door hid the building from the street. I went in to make sure everything was cool while the others grabbed bags and belongings from the van.

Now, if you're ever in Eilat and have some money in your pocket and want a nice hotel experience, there are plenty of great places, believe me. Try something down by the water—it's beautiful there. *But,* if you're on a serious budget and don't mind rough-around-the-edges and a good dose of adventure off the tourist path, then the Sunset's your place. The only word I can think to describe it is *trippy.* Think David Lynch meets Jack Kerouac, and then toss in a little Indiana Jones for flavor. Stepping into the courtyard, I found myself in another world, far removed from the dusty, desert-town street. Tree branches stretched overhead. Orange, purple, green, and blue lights splashed everywhere. The sculpted, cavelike walls had shapes molded over them—tree roots, branches, and tribal stone carvings. Low, built-in couches and tables bordered the wide patio with hookahs lining a shelf behind them. A big, curly haired dog cracked one eye open at me from its place on a wicker chair. Water dripped. I half expected to hear the theme song from *Twin Peaks* waft out from somewhere.

To my left, thick, varnished beams held up a shade structure. Beneath it, a young African girl manned a bar. She just stood there with arms crossed, leaning against a post, watching me. Her dress hung loosely from the straps over her thin shoulders. I smiled at her and said hello. She offered a bored blink and said nothing. I tried again, telling her I'd emailed ahead for a reservation. She said something in Hebrew. I asked her if she spoke English. She sighed and gave a shout toward the back. A male growl replied.

Enter Avi—owner, designer, and builder of the Sunset. He emerged a bit disheveled, hair askew, sandals, baggy pants, and an old tank top. He barked at the girl and, with a wave, shooed her scurrying away. Then he turned to me.

"What?" he snapped.

"Hi, I booked a reservation online—"

"I don't know anything about it," he interrupted, turning as if to head back into the shadows.

All I could think about at that moment were my tired travelers outside. "No, I'm telling you I booked online. I paid for four rooms on the website. My group is outside with our bags."

Looking doubtful, he weighed the situation. He shouted, and the African girl came back. He said something in Hebrew. The girl sighed, gave me a look as if I'd insulted her family, then disappeared again.

He sighed and shook his head. You'd have thought I'd asked him to cure the common cold or help me move. "She'll get some rooms ready." He held out his hand. "Cash or credit card?"

"Like I told you, I paid online. The rooms are already paid for."

He turned the volume up from three to eight. "And I told you! Cash *or credit card!*"

We squared off. "Look, man. I paid for *four* rooms. I don't know what to tell you."

Verbal sparring went on for quite a while, but we eventually worked it out.

Now, Avi—whom you just met—is what you'd call . . . let's just say *colorful.* The poor guy gets a pretty bad rap in the hotel reviews. True, he yells a lot, especially if you want him to get out of bed in the morning to unlock the gate and let you out. (This request is apparently unacceptable.) But spend a little time with the guy, ask him about his motel, and he'll warm up. He loves the place. You get the feeling it's the guests he's not crazy about. I don't blame him. People can be a trial sometimes. Truth be told, I'd probably feel the same. Keep an open mind. He's an alright guy.

Bags unloaded, rooms settled and arranged, we climbed back into the van and headed for the waterfront lights and food. The city vibrated with life; it was a calliope of color. We were all a little falafel and shawarma-ed out, so the aroma of grilling meat coming from the Burger Ranch had us circling like sharks drawn to blood. Burger Ranch—the only place I've ever been where you can order a hamburger the size of a pizza. Brilliant. Let me tell you, when you're starving, the Sliceburger ranks right up there with the PillCam, USB drives, and Waze GPS. Never underestimate the genius of the Israelis.

Dance clubs, restaurants, and a waterfront midway—nighttime

Eilat throbs with noise and energy, a playground for the young and young at heart. Out past the promenade the noise quieted to a dull, rhythmic thump as I stood in the dark, knee-deep in the Red Sea. Ships lay at anchor on the calm water. Across the way, the lights of Lawrence of Arabia's Aqaba winked from just over the Jordanian border. I dialed home on my cell. It felt like heaven to hear my wife's voice.

Later, back at the Sunset, no one felt ready to turn in. So we gathered some chairs and camped awhile beneath the patio lanterns, talking and letting the day slip away at its own pace. In a far corner, Avi sat on a worn couch chain-smoking and petting the curly haired dog. His cigarette glowed in the dark, faded, then glowed again. On a whim, I asked him to join us. I figured he'd either decline or ignore me altogether. Glow . . . fade . . . glow. At length he shrugged, lit a fresh one with the tip of his last, eased his lanky frame up, and dragged a chair over. The dog followed lazily and then sank to the concrete beside him.

Conversation, slow out of the station, gradually picked up steam, and Avi mellowed. We asked him about his motel, then about his life and history. He humored us, smoking and walking his mind back through the desert and the decades, his words laced with the struggles and joys of carving out a life in that hard land. I knew he still held his cards close to his vest—there were things he wouldn't give up to outsiders—but we took what he offered. After all, this was history unwritten, stuff you couldn't Google or watch on a PBS documentary. He talked through at least half a pack, and we lost track of time. At last, after the moon dropped beneath the patio wall, Avi stubbed out his last butt, saluted a goodnight, and headed for his room. The curly haired dog followed close on his heels.

The group left early the next morning for their Petra excursion. I found myself with a free day. I gassed up the van, grabbed some truck-stop coffee and chocolate croissants—the best in the world (the best croissants, not coffee)—and headed south along the western edge of the Red Sea. After a few miles I pulled a U-turn close to the Egyptian border and cruised the beaches looking for a likely spot to pass the day. Resorts, bars, and dive shops lined nearly every foot of the water's edge.

The Red Sea's crystal-clear water and abundant sea life is a diver's paradise and draws scuba enthusiasts from around the world, but I wasn't in a diving frame of mind. After days and days of travel, I just wanted my own little piece of beach and some rest. I found a parking lot with some vacant spaces and a sign promising beach access through the thatched-roof pub. The girl at the bar looked me up and down as though I had three eyes and had just parked my spaceship outside. But when I bought a couple bottles of water and gave her a good tip, I guess she decided I was okay. She only spoke Hebrew but somehow understood my question and pointed the way to the beach. Once out on the sand, I understood her surprised reaction to my presence. This was no American hangout. Pure Israeli all the way. My baggy board shorts were all by their lonesome in a sea of speedos. I found an empty beach chair, downed half my water, and leaned back for a nap. A group of elderly guys—you guessed it: speedos and shirtless—played dominos around a table. Families frolicked, children laughed, and I slept. After a while I swam a little, then slept again.

I woke up to see a rail-thin, very feminine-looking man standing in front of me slathering himself head to toe with some kind of silver, sparkling sunscreen. He made a serious production of it. By the end of the application, he looked like a glittery Tin Man from *The Wizard of Oz*. He sauntered ankle-deep into the water and somehow managed to get himself onto a beach raft without getting his impressive pompadour wet. Propped on one elbow, he used his free hand to paddle back and forth, up and down the beach. Poor guy was dying to be noticed, but everyone just went on with their vacationing. In the end he gave up and flopped onto a beach towel. I wondered about his story, but I was too tired to ask.

By late afternoon I was pretty crispy—but not as crispy as some of the speedo guys. I headed back to the street in front of the Sunset, our rendezvous spot. The group hadn't come back yet. It was past checkout time, and I wasn't supposed to be there, but I really didn't feel like waiting in the hot van. I took my life in my hands and pushed through the wooden door.

All quiet in Twin Peaks. True to form, Avi lounged and scratched the curly haired dog behind the ears. The young African girl rested her elbows on the bar and watched a woman sing a Middle Eastern melody on the TV. I asked Avi if I could hang for a while. He squinted and paused, then shook his finger-scissored cigarette at me, speaking in Hebrew. By the tone and the look on his face, I had no doubts I was about to get tossed out on my ear. I held my ground. In the end, he sighed and waved me to a chair. I sat. He went back to scratching the dog, his thoughts far away. He never said another word.

Yeah, Avi's an alright guy.

My friends finally made it back. We drove through the night to make a flight in Tel Aviv. Somewhere in the middle of the Negev, we stopped to look at the riot of stars. They vibrated in the sky and overflowed to the horizon, so bright I felt I could hear them if I listened hard enough. A billion Tin Men paddling through their inky sea above a world distracted by the glow of a phone screen. The van engine ticked as it cooled, loud in the desert stillness. I thought about a God who could imagine a sky like that. Could fill it to overflowing with moons and suns and planets—celestial bodies dancing side by side with an African girl's dreams. It hit me then. I knew in that moment that this place wasn't lifeless at all. It was, in fact, filled to the brim. Pressed full with God and His radical star-drenched love.

He imagines universes. He paints the sky with His fingertips.

And He smiles down on a crusty motel owner, an African girl, and a curly haired dog.

CHAPTER 3

Knocking on the Gates of Hell

Farms, wineries, and nature reserves marked the drive up through the Hula Valley. The psalmist's poetically dewy Mount Hermon rose on the horizon, marking the farthest northern tip of the country, where Lebanon sits to the west and Syria to the east. The dew still gathers up there on the old man's head. And rain. And even snow. In fact, the Mount Hermon Ski Resort is in operation January through March. You can slide down a biblical-landmark mountain balanced between two countries while Russian bombs dust the horizon. Not your usual ski trip.

All that high-up water eventually works its way down through the layers of rock, emerges at the base of the mountain, and forms springs that jump-start the Jordan River.

Banias is a beautiful spot.

We parked and climbed out of the van, stretching our legs. My friends headed across the lot to the mom-and-pop snack shop, looking for something cold to drink while I walked over to the little ticket office that marked the trailhead leading down to the Banias Waterfall. Sun high, it was already hot but still a good day for hiking.

The man on the other side of the window blinked at me through his glasses. "You are American or Canadian?" His accent was thick Hebrew.

"American."

"Ah. So, how is America today?"

"I haven't been there in a while. I'm not sure," I said. "But Israel's definitely nice."

"Of course it is. Israel is always nice," he said.

True story. Blue sky, birds singing, the only thing putting a damper on the day was the ripe odor of the dairy cows coming from the kibbutz next door. And even that wasn't all that bad.

"You have been here before?" he said.

"A few times."

"Here? To the north?"

"I love the north. It's my favorite part of Israel."

"Not Jerusalem? Most Americans like Jerusalem the best."

"Oh, I do like Jerusalem. But the north's my favorite. It's quiet. Not as crowded."

"Yes, most of the time it's quiet."

I thought about Lebanon and Syria a stone's throw away. And the land mine warning signs along the border road. "You've had your hard seasons."

"A few." He looked over our passes, noting holes punched for some of the other places we'd already visited. "Americans don't usually come to the falls."

"I imagine the bigger tours don't have a lot of extra time. And not everyone is in hiking shape."

"That's true. We don't offer . . . what do you call those moving stairs?"

"An escalator?"

He smiled. "Yes. We don't have that thing. It's warm today. You have plenty of water?"

"We're all set." It would be cooler down by the falls.

Looking out at the dry grass, you'd never guess a clear river rushed and galloped through lush green just down the hill or that waterfalls plunged into sun-dappled pools. I remembered my last hike there. I'd been surprised to see all the fish leaping upstream, silver bellies flashing like the salmon back home. Jewish tradition says this is where the psalmist penned the line "Deep calls to deep in the roar of your waterfalls" (Psalm 42:7 NIV). I could imagine it to be true.

The window guy began marking our passes with his hole punch. "But you are not with a tour?"

"Not really. Just a few of us traveling together. We rented a van in Tel Aviv, and now we're staying down in Migdal for a few days. We came up here today to hike and see the falls. Then go over to the ruins."

He paused midpunch and studied me for a second. "You are not afraid to come to Israel?"

"I'm here, aren't I? Do you think I shouldn't be?"

Another smile. "Don't you watch CNN? CNN says you should be afraid to be here."

"I've learned not to believe everything I see. Especially news where Israel is concerned. Are you afraid to come to America?"

He laughed. "Of course! America is a very dangerous country. Every day there is a shooting there. America is much more dangerous than Israel."

I looked behind me. No line. In fact, the parking lot was practically empty. And the conversation was taking an interesting turn. I leaned forward on the counter. "What about the war over the border? And the Palestinian violence? And Jewish aggression? Isn't that dangerous? According to the news, you all are trying to kill each other day and night, right?"

My new friend turned to another young man sitting in the back of the office reading a book. "Hey, you want to kill me?"

The young man looked up. "Are you talking to me?"

"Who else? Yes, you."

"No, not today."

"You will want to kill me tomorrow?"

A shrug. "You never know. We'll see."

"You're Palestinian?" I asked the book guy.

"Yes. I live in Buq'ata."

"See?" my friend said. "A Jew and a Palestinian locked in a box all day, and we don't kill each other. We are friends. We should call CNN."

"Or the UN. They don't seem to like you much. Maybe they could learn something."

"The *United Nothing* couldn't find the Lebanese border, let alone Banias."

"I have to ask, if you two can get along, why can't the rest of Israel?" I knew it was much too complicated a question for a ticket line, but I was curious about how they might answer.

Book Guy said, "We are not politicians or religious leaders, are we? Most Jews and Palestinians live together peacefully every day."

Pass Puncher added, "We are only people. We just want to live our lives with our families. To be left alone." He pointed to the east.

"Listen, many days you can hear the bombs in Syria. For what? Money? Power? Religion?"

I didn't hear Syrian bombs. Only the faint sound of water rushing down in the valley. "I don't blame you."

"You are Christian?" Pass Puncher asked.

"Absolutely."

"They say Jesus came here, to Banias. Did you know that?"

"Yes. Caesarea Philippi. It's in the New Testament. Do you believe in Jesus?"

"That He existed? Of course. Everyone knows He existed. Even the Muslims. But Jesus was a Jew."

"A Jew, yes. But you don't believe He was the Messiah?"

"How can I? I am a Jew."

"Lots of Jews believed Jesus was the Messiah. Lots of Jews still do."

"You are a Christian." He indicated his friend with a jerk of his thumb. "He is Muslim. I am a Jew. We all believe what we believe."

"Okay."

Another grin. "Maybe His ghost is still here, yes? Maybe you'll see Him today."

"I believe He rose from the dead, remember? How could He be a ghost if He's still alive?"

He shrugged. "One day we'll see, yes?"

"One day we definitely will. So, we have a Christian, a Jew, and a Muslim not killing each other. Is there hope for Middle East peace, then?"

He handed me back the punched park passes with a smile. "You never know. Call CNN. Welcome to Banias. Enjoy the hike."

His partner had already gone back to his book.

We did enjoy the hike. My new friend waved as we exited the trail. We bought cold bottles of water and cooled off at a shaded table under the watchful gaze of several friendly faced dairy cows.

Afterward, we drove a half mile or so upstream to the ruins of the New Testament community of Caesarea Philippi. One of my absolutely favorite places. A must-see in Israel.

The springs at the base of Mount Hermon are nothing new. And in the Middle East—like everywhere on the planet—water means life. Settlements existed at these springs even before Abraham came through after God called him to head west out of Ur. During Alexander the Great's Hellenistic period a few centuries before Jesus, the area became a hub for worshipping the god Pan (as in Peter) and began to be referred to as *Paneas*. (This was long before Walt Disney gave the kid a green hat, tights, a fairy-girlfriend, and threw a dash of pixie dust over the whole deal.)

Caesarea Philippi, Paneas, Banias—the whole name thing gets a little confusing, but Israel is like that. In this case, the name *Paneas* worked just fine in the beginning, but when the Romans took over a place, they had a habit of running around renaming everything after Caesar. As you can imagine, naming everything after one guy probably got confusing, so when Herod the Great's son Philip dubbed the place *Caesarea,* he tagged *Philippi* on the end. Whether out of ego or to keep the post office from mixing up mail sacks is unclear. Although *Caesarea Philippi* stuck for a while and is prominent in the New Testament, at some point the name eventually faded back to *Paneas* which, in turn, the Arabs morphed into *Banias*, the name that stands to this day.

For me, the cultic ruin of Caesarea Philippi is one of the most impactful sites in Israel. So I'm always surprised to pull into the parking lot and find the place practically empty. For starters, it's beautiful. David's dew wells up from the ground in wide, staggered pools beneath cliffs dotted with intricately carved niches that once held statues representing the gods (notice the little "g") of this word. In Jesus's day a massive temple dedicated to Pan extended from the cliff face. Originally the spring gushed from a cave behind the temple. The historian Josephus, in his *Antiquities of the Jews*, claimed the depths of the fountain could not be measured. Early worshippers considered it a doorway to the underworld. They called it the Gates of Hell. Sound familiar?

It was to this oasis of beauty and wealth and misplaced religious piety that Jesus brought His disciples. A long walk by any stretch. Why? Because there, in that hub of worldly, demonic worship, He wanted to ask them a question.

He put it to them directly: "Boys, who do men say that I—the Son of Man—am?"

Some hemming and hawing occurred at that point. I can picture the group looking around at the majestic setting. The water. The trees. The huge white Gates of Hell temple. Beautifully carved statues and idols everywhere. Had to be an imposing sight.

"One of the prophets," said one, finally.

"Elijah," said another.

"John the Baptist."

Then Jesus did what He always did—what He still does if we care to listen. He cut straight to the heart of the matter. "But who do *you* say that I am?"

What an incredible, angel-rejoicing moment when Peter (not Pan) stepped up and said, "You are the Christ, the Son of the living God" (Matthew 16:13–20).

Standing in that place wrecks me every time. I hear Him whisper, "But who do *you* say that I am?"

"You know me, Jesus. I'm with Peter. You are the Christ. You are my Lord."

Blessed are you . . .

Yes, without a doubt—I am blessed. Beyond anything I can describe with words.

Can you imagine that moment two thousand years ago? I promise, you would if you stood in that place. Jesus, Son of the Living God, pointed up at that magnificent temple and said, "Blessed are you, Simon Bar-Jonah, for flesh and blood has not revealed this to you, but My Father who is in heaven. . . . You are Peter, and on this rock I will build My church, and the Gates of Hades shall not prevail against it" (Matthew 16:17–18).

Jesus said that the *Gates of Hell*—that intimidating tower, representing every false god, all the wealth, all the power of every worldly system—didn't stand a chance against the might and the love of the living God.

It still doesn't.

I will build My church . . .

I hear people complain about the church today. And, frankly, more often than not they're right. Not all, but many—and more every day—of our modern church franchises operate in a weird ghetto of fads and waves and programs. Usually with a carnival-barker-frontman-CEO tickling ears (or even using sound doctrine) as a tool to yank dollars out of the pockets of seat-warming tithing units. And sadly, much too often those dollars aren't allocated to the work of Christ on earth but are instead "diversified" into side businesses and second homes. Modern Pharisees professing righteousness but devoid of real Love. Behind the smoke and mirrors, their lives rarely back up their well-practiced lip service.

But that's *man's* church. And man will answer for those things when required.

Conversely—and joyfully—the church that *Jesus* is actively building in the hearts and lives of His followers is a beautiful and eternal thing. It will stand because He is faithful even when we're faithless. He is loving even when we are unlovely.

He is God. We are not.

And I'm glad.

My group and I sat for a while, lingering in the shade and the echo of His voice, reluctant to move on. Sometimes it's better not to rush. To slow down. To take the time to listen. Once, lifetimes ago, Caesarea Philippi was an evil place, filled with devils. Blustering gods of nothing. And the Bright Morning Star swept them away with a word and a thought.

He's like that, you know, if you give Him the chance.

After a while we walked on, following the river. We stopped at the van, but the cool dew of Hermon flowed on, swirling, babbling toward the Jordan, marking a lazy path through lost memories and shards of shattered gods before plunging down beneath a shack where a Jew and an Arab and once in a while a Christian (but not Jesus's ghost) spend long, blue-sky days. Where the soft winds of Lebanon rattle through the olive trees, ripple the dry grass, and whisper, *Who do you say that I am?*

CHAPTER 4

Broken Bread— and a Bad Day for Turkeys

In Middle Eastern culture, something we Westerners take for granted—the simple act of eating together—is more than a big deal. Breaking bread together is a warmhearted and joyful party. It's family, friends, and an I've-got-your-back commitment.

In the Middle East breaking bread is a love story.

I've had a lot of great meals in that corner of the world. But it's funny. One of my more memorable bread-breaking experiences happened half a world away from the sunny sands of King Solomon and Lawrence of Arabia.

It was in Boise, Idaho, to be exact.

I'd been invited to partner in some ministry dates with a brother of mine—Michael Paul, an Iraqi Christian. A convert from Islam, Michael had an incredible testimony of conviction and conversion. He'd been tortured close to the point of death many times for his unwavering dedication to Jesus.

I was happy for the chance to partner with him. The events went well. I did some concert work, and my friend shared his testimony and encouraged listeners in the strength of the Lord. The last day in Boise, Michael insisted we have a meal at a place he knew. Food—sounded good to me.

Boise is home to a large population of Iraqi refugees, and Michael, magnanimous personality that he is, seemed to know every single one of them. We drove to a strip mall—signs all in Arabic—and parked in front of what looked like a little grocery store.

"Hey, man, I think this is a grocery store," I said, figuring he'd mixed up his locations.

"Yes, it is a store."

"We're gonna eat in a grocery store?"

Michael spoke with affection and patience. "*Habibi*, you don't trust?"

A loaded question if I'd ever heard one. A word about Michael. This is a brother who charges into life headlong and lets the chips fall where they may. He has *no problem* telling anyone and everyone within earshot about Jesus. I've gotten saved five times in an hour just having coffee with the guy. Church, doctor's office, barroom, walking down the street—you name it, within five minutes he's friends with everyone. And without fail, just at the moment I think he's about to get killed, the homeless guy, hard-core lesbian, atheist, Hells Angel—whoever is in Michael's crosshairs—breaks into a smile and gives him a hug. This is no exaggeration. Michael is disarming, not because he works at it or tries to be, but because he just can't seem to contain the enormity of God's love inside that scarred and broken body.

I opened the door. "No, I absolutely don't trust you at all. Let's go in."

Five or six Arab men loitered and lounged in the store's cool interior. They definitely didn't look too happy to see us. At least to see me, Mr. Scotch-Irish.

True to form, Michael blasted into conversation as soon as we walked in. All in machine-gun Arabic, of course. I had no idea what was going on. Just watched the whole thing like a fast-forward racquetball match. It rolled on awhile. Heated, then friendly, warm, heated again. . . . Typical Arab interaction. After a while Michael shook hands with the counter guy and motioned me to follow. I felt several pairs of eyes track me as we tailed the man I assumed to be the proprietor through a curtain to a side room with a few tables and chairs. He motioned us to sit. We did.

More back-and-forth staccato Arabic. Then our host headed back through some doors into what looked to be a kitchen.

Through the open curtain the loungers continued to watch us.

"What are they looking at?" I said.

"You. What else? I'm Iraqi."

"They don't look happy."

Michael shrugged.

"So is this an actual restaurant?"

"It is for us."

I indicated our audience. "Are they Christian?"

"Of course not! They are Muslim."

"That's just super."

We talked awhile. I tried to ignore the audience. At length food started arriving.

Then kept arriving.

Then arrived some more.

Hummus, pita, dolma, kebab, rice—plate after plate came.

"Now you will pray to thank God for the food, *habibi*," Michael said. "Go ahead."

"Me?"

"Of course."

He sensed my hesitation. "Why you don't want to pray?"

"It might have something to do with the fact that we're sitting in the middle of a terrorist cell straight out of *24*."

He laughed. Our watchers didn't.

I prayed. I *was* truly thankful for this brother of mine. Prayer finished—and encouraged by the fact I had not been riddled with bullets—I said, "So, are they eating with us?"

"No. You and me."

I pointed to the piles of plates. "Then why all the food, man?"

He lit up with his Michael smile. "Because you and I are brothers!" He waved a hand around. "And they love me!"

And such is the importance of eating together both in the Arab and Jewish cultures. Something that is most often lost in our Western fast-food, gather-around-the-television mentality.

You are my brother. You are welcome at my table. I've got your back.

We ate till we could hold no more. Some of the best food I've *ever* had. A lot more Arabic flew around that room that day. The loungers joined the conversation. Or the debate—I'm not sure. I wasn't surprised when they all shook our hands as we left. This was Michael, after all. Back in the car I asked him, "So, apostle Paul, are they all Christians now?"

He dropped the gearshift into reverse and shrugged. "They will be soon. My Jesus will rescue them."

The cultural aspect of breaking bread has been a favorite part of my knocking around the Holy Land. It doesn't hurt that the food is off-the-chart amazing. In fact, travel Israel and you very well may be ruined for food anywhere else. I hear that a lot. It's a place where you don't have to wonder if it's fresh, because all of it is. You don't go out of your way for organic—everything *is* organic. The Israelis are agricultural geniuses, so fruits and vegetables are always straight from the fields and extremely flavorful.

Let me touch on a few delights you may have heard of and a few you probably haven't.

First, *hummus*. Yes, we've all bought it at Costco along with a ninety-pound bag of pita chips, but let me tell you, it doesn't compare. Hummus in the Middle East is a must.

And *falafel*. Some people love it, some hate it, and some scratch their heads and wonder why they're eating a main dish that isn't meat. Personally, I could live on falafel when I'm in Israel. Ground-up chickpeas, rolled into a ball and deep-fried. Little chunks of happiness. A couple of years ago I saw a hole-in-the-wall stand a few blocks off Yafo Street in Jerusalem. It had a sign that bragged Best Falafel in Israel. I bought a falafel pita and took a few bites. Then—oh, man— I shook the guy's hand. I've been back three or four times since. Then again, it's hard to find bad falafel in the Holy Land.

Israel is somewhat unique in the fact that, like the United States, it's a cultural crossroads and melting pot. This lends—in a good way—to a lot of different culinary influences. Spices from the Middle East, North Africa, the Mediterranean. *Schnitzel, kabob, baklava, halva.*

A friend and I ducked into a little café in the Galilee region early one morning, and I experienced for the first time *shakshuka*, a traditional Israeli breakfast. This is something you generally won't find at the hotels catering to tourists, but if you have the opportunity to get out on your own, don't miss it. Usually served in a small skillet, eggs are baked in tomato sauce, garlic, peppers, chili, and other spices. It's a happy *must*. I'm getting hungry writing this.

But there's an exception to every rule.

Let me add a little downer here in my happy lovefest for Israeli food.

A while back I took a small group—Pastor Jim and his family and friends—around Israel. Seven of us total. We were in the far north checking out Nimrod Fortress for much of the day. Then we headed back down the Jordan Valley to Migdal, where we were staying. I don't remember what we'd done for lunch, but I recall it was getting late by the time we got back down south. We were all starting to feel like that old cartoon where the fat guy sees the skinny guy as a hot dog, and the skinny guy sees the fat guy as a hamburger. I'd spotted a little restaurant back off the highway down the road from our place. It looked quick and reasonable, so we figured we might as well give it a try. Not many people inside, and the owner—definitely more hamburger than hot dog—lit up when he saw our party walk in. He chatted us up with a mixture of rapid-fire Hebrew and very broken English as he led us to a long table in the corner.

Water pitchers arrived. Other assorted drinks. We looked over the menus while the proprietor hovered and suggested, a benevolent UFO. We ordered a few things. Our host, as any good host does, clucked his tongue indicating he knew better and took it upon himself to augment the order. Tabouli, hummus, tangy garlic sauce with pita appeared. Then rice, schnitzel, shawarma, kebab, and piles of stuff I didn't recognize. More host hovering. Smiling and nodding and insisting we try everything.

Now, Pastor Jim is not a small guy at six-foot-six, and he likes to eat. So do I. So did a few others on the trip. We made a pretty good dent in the feast. Late in the meal I saw Jim perusing the menu again.

"You can't be hungry," I said.

"More curious than hungry," he said "because they have turkey testicles."

"Lovely."

We all agreed this was not good news for turkeys.

Our host was all ears. "Yes, yes, testicles!" (You have to hear this phrase in a Hebrew accent.)

I could tell in that moment this wasn't going to end well.

Pastor Jim is from North Carolina. I can still hear his drawl. "Okay, we gotta try 'em."

"No. No, we really don't," I said. I've honestly never meant anything more in my entire life.

"Yup. Gotta try 'em," Jim said.

"Yes, yes! Testicles!" our host said, clapping. I think he almost danced.

Let me offer you the perspective of a guy with some miles under his wheels. There is not one situation—*ever*—when *Yes, yes, testicles!* is something you want to hear come out of the mouth of a little, round restaurant owner. Or anyone else, for that matter.

The owner darted off. Five minutes later he was back, beaming with pride. He plopped in the middle of the table a steaming, foul-smelling plate filled with what I figured must be the result of several very upset turkeys. I didn't move a muscle. Not even when a few staff came over to watch the stupid-Americans-eat-testicles show.

I squinted at the little fried fellas. "You're really gonna eat that?" I asked finally.

Jim didn't seem at all fazed. He forked one. "Yup," he said. "You?"

I don't consider myself a picky eater. I've traveled a lot in my life. I've jumped into many a questionable culinary pool without complaint. But a guy's got to draw the line someplace.

The bad news for me—and the turkey, I guess—is testicles didn't constitute that line. I have to admit curiosity (or manly pride) got the better of me.

No, my friends, turkey testicles are not good.

Although you wouldn't know it by watching Big Jim. He finished the plate to the delight of our host and the staff.

No, testicles aren't good. But breaking bread together is very good. We sat long. We laughed, we talked, we listened.

We even made new friends.

Not one of them a turkey.

CHAPTER 5

Parting the Black Sea

L ife has its ups and downs. We all know it's true because we've all been there. I have a dark suspicion the earthly journey of a musician or writer—of any kind of artist, for that matter—has a way of cranking the needle way past both ends of the scale. That's okay. To get where we want to go, it's a ride we're obliged to take. You see, the good stuff is rarely birthed in comfort. Ups and downs. Ups and downs . . .

Sometimes—but don't ask me how this works—we even manage to fly and fall at the same time. Los Angeles in the mid-eighties was one of those stretches for me. Creating, writing, playing every grungy dive in the city with my friends and brothers was pure mountaintop stuff. Starving to death while we did it? Not so great.

Those were broke and hungry days. So when a couple of guys from the next apartment down knocked on my door and asked if I wanted to make some money, I jumped.

Now, let me paint a picture. These weren't the *bake you a pie and welcome you to the neighborhood* kind of neighbors. More the L.A. metal-scene set. But they were nice enough guys and, luckily, the job wasn't picking up some suspicious package from a Russian warehouse or bumping anybody off. Instead, on a bright Sunday morning, three or four of us piled into an old Lincoln and headed for the Exposition Park neighborhood in downtown L.A. We parked next to the Los Angeles Coliseum. One of the guys knew a guy. . . . A couple hours later I was officially hawking Cokes up and down miles and miles— and miles!—of concrete stairs while the L.A. Raiders took on the New York Jets.

I worked a couple more games and made a little money. Then the concessions manager announced we'd be hosting Bruce Springsteen's *Born in the USA* tour four straight nights: extra Coke schleppers needed. My metal friends couldn't care less about Springsteen. Me? I stepped forward and saluted.

Raiders games were loud and energetic. Once in a while fights broke out, adding a little extra entertainment. People yelled, baked in the sun, bought a lot of Cokes. But Springsteen, on Night #1, took the meaning of *crowd* to a whole new level. Stands packed, field packed, a hundred thousand bodies gathered to worship at the altar of The Boss. They screamed, smoked a lot of pot, and, yup, bought a lot of Cokes. I emptied my Coke racks several times that first night.

Night #2 I was so sucked into the music, I only sold a couple of racks. Night #3, the same. Night #4, the manager handed me a floor pass so I could sell on the field. My sales were way down, and he thought I'd have better luck down there. Bad move for soda sales. I emptied exactly one rack so I wouldn't have to carry the thing. I think I sold the last Coke to Pierce Brosnan (aka Remington Steele at the time), which I thought was cool. I remember he wore a jacket with a big eagle on the back.

When Bruce took the stage, I looked up and around from where

I stood, somewhere near the fifty-yard line. An ocean of people, united in music, shook the L.A. sky. Coke-free, I ditched the metal rack and headed straight to the front row. The fans up there were loose and friendly and didn't mind my being there. For the next four hours, a great American songwriter and poet blew my mind.

Two-thirds of the way through the show, the band left, and Bruce picked up an acoustic guitar. He started in on a cover of Woody Guthrie's "This Land Is Your Land." The crowd fell silent. It felt to me like one massive organism holding its breath. With the last chord the place erupted. One voice, one mind.

God spoke over Babel, "They are one people. . . . And nothing that they propose to do will now be impossible for them" (Genesis 11:6 ESV).

And on Day #5 my manager spoke over me: my Coke-hawking career had come to an end. I figured it was a good trade. . . .

It was the first time in my young life I'd truly experienced mass unity. A powerful ability built into the human race for the purpose of worshipping our Creator. A trait that has so often jumped track.

The Raiders had nothing on Bruce. But Bruce wasn't even a drop in the bucket next to the March 2, 2014, Haredim protest on the Jerusalem streets. A protest my friend Pastor Ben Ortize and I accidentally found ourselves smack-dab in the middle of on that lovely evening in Israel.

We'd risen early that day and ridden the Jerusalem Light Rail the two or three miles from our hotel to the Jaffa Gate. Sunday is a great day to explore the Old City on foot, and we spent most of our time doing just that. In the heat of the afternoon, we descended narrow, steep stairs into the Armenian Tavern. In this cool, dark little place tucked deep beneath the stone streets of the Armenian Quarter, a young waiter showed us to a table in the corner. Behind an ornately carved wooden bar, an old man with a million stories on his face smoked a cigarette and leaned over a newspaper. He didn't look up. American pop music floated out from the kitchen.

Ben is a good traveling companion. Curious about roads less traveled. A brilliant thinker and a fascinating guy. We took our time, lingering over good food and conversation. At length we decided to call it a day and head back to the hotel. We climbed the stairs, headed past Christ Church and King David's Citadel. Close to the Jaffa Gate, we overheard a passerby say that he was rushing to catch the Light Rail before it was shut down. *Strange,* I thought. *The Light Rail usually runs till late at night.*

"Why are they shutting it down?" Ben asked.

The reply came back steeped in a Middle Eastern accent, but I thought I heard the word *protest* somewhere in there.

We decided we'd better scoot. We hustled through the Jaffa Gate and toward the train stop on Jaffa Street. Sure enough, we found the train parked and empty.

"Did you hear anything this morning about a protest?" Ben asked.

I hadn't, but then again neither of us had made it a habit to keep up with local news.

All public transportation was shut down. Period. No choice but to walk. Anyway, we figured our hotel was a straight shot. Only a few miles up Jaffa Street. No big deal.

Jaffa Street is a great place to explore on foot. It's been a main thruway in Jerusalem for thousands of years and still is today. Shops, cafés, stores of every kind are always busy. Side streets offer endless exploration and unique opportunities. When the sun disappears,

Jaffa becomes one of the centers of Jerusalem nightlife. Street musicians fill the night with sound. Normally it's a bustling, joyful place.

But as Ben and I walked that evening, something seemed off. We both felt it. More than a heaviness. An *intensity* was in the air.

"Does it seem like there are a lot more Orthodox here than usual?" Ben asked.

I said it did.

It was true. And all men. They gathered in small groups at first, but soon more—a lot more—began filtering in from the side streets.

We picked up our pace.

The Haredim. This term covers a broad swath of theologically, politically, and socially conservative ultra-Orthodox Jews. They are arguably the most recognizable subset of people in Israel. Long black coats, flat-brimmed black hats, and beards for the men. Long dresses, modest stockings, and covered heads for the women. In an intricate and multilayered society, the Haredim are a controversial lot. Practicing constant study of the Torah and maintaining strict reverence for it—both the written and oral law—the Haredim believe themselves to be the most genuine and authentic when it comes to being Jewish. They are extremely dedicated and uncompromising in matters of faith.

And great photo ops for rubbernecking tourists.

But a sightseer asking to take a picture with an ultra-Orthodox is likely in for a rude awakening. I once had a woman traveling with me who suffered from a bad knee. In pain, she sat down to rest for a minute on a plastic chair on one of the Old City streets.

Wrong chair.

She was stunned when a Haredim shouted, spat on her, and chased her off with a shaking fist.

You see, to protect their way of life from worldly influence, the Haredim try very hard to avoid personal contact with outsiders, both Jew and non-Jew. They live in cloistered communities. They're opposed to all secular education, and very few of the men hold any type of job, choosing instead to devote their time to prayer and the study of Scripture.

The apostle Paul had a thought on this subject of work a couple thousand years ago. He told the Thessalonians, "Hey, man, you don't work you don't eat" (Buck Standard Version). This being the case, Haredim communities are plagued with extreme poverty. Large families rely heavily on state programs and various charities to survive. Thus the controversy. Talk to the everyday guy on the street, and you'll find the majority of taxpaying Israelis tending to lean into Paul's line of thinking.

As of March 2, 2014, another hot button of contention was the Haredim's continuing exemption from military conscription. In Israel, laws demand military service. Three years for men, two for women. With much of the world chomping at the bit to literally wipe the country off the map, it's an all-hands-on-deck situation. For generations the Haredim considered their life of study and prayer reasonable substitutionary service. But, as old Bobby Zimmerman put it, *the times they are a-changin'*. And with legislation on the table to draft Haredim men into mandatory military service, the boys in black decided nothing doing. It was time to protest.

As Ben and I walked on, the intensity built—and it built fast. Orthodox men poured onto Jaffa Street now from every lane and alley. Signs held high. Chants and shouts. Another half mile, and the only thing in either direction was a sea of black hats and beards.

The air was electric. It became harder and harder to press through the crowd. I'll admit, by this time I was feeling a little nervous. I tried my best to ignore the fact that Ben and I were the only two non-black-robed-but-cowboy-hat-wearing *gringos* in the middle of a high-agitation zone.

Ben appeared fairly calm. I figured I'd at least fake it.

We walked on.

Near Jerusalem's famous Bridge of Strings, a young boy, seven or eight, long curls hanging down the side of his face, waved at us from a stone wall. The little guy received a sharp rebuke from an older man. I waved back anyway. The kid looked around carefully. When he was sure he was unobserved, he waved again and added a million-dollar grin. One thing I've come across in my travels and loved is—no matter the country, language, or culture—kids will be kids. With the boy's smile I felt a tiny glimmer of that first-garden innocence, precious in the sight of the Lord. A candle flame of hope, out of place in that roiling, angry sea of black.

Maybe it was the kid, maybe just American ignorance, but I wasn't nervous anymore. I climbed partway up a light pole for a better view. Bullhorns stabbed the air with nasal-toned urgency. An orchestrated thunder of voices shook the walls, pounded the air, and vibrated through my body as the light pole answered their cry with harmonic sympathy. The voice, the soul of man fighting to be heard, right or wrong, in all its anger, urgency, and righteous desperation.

No, Springsteen had nothing on the Haredim.

Later, I read the gathering was estimated to be close to half a million souls—the largest gathering of Jewish men in recorded history.

(Five times as many as my Springsteen concert.)

Plus two curious and slightly nervous Gentiles.

I remember in that moment—hanging there on my light pole,

suspended between heaven and broken humanity—feeling sad. A people trapped in a system of law. A people in love with their suffering. Adored by their Creator, yet bunching their shoulders and turning up their collars against the warm Breath of Grace as if it were a chill north wind.

In the end this was not our place. Not our fight. I climbed down, and Ben and I pushed on toward our hotel. Not far now. As we walked, I turned and looked again for our young friend on the wall. Maybe one more smile, one small piece of sunlight—of hope— I could carry with me out of that sea of black.

But the boy was gone.

CHAPTER 6

The Beginning Is Near

Musician's hours aren't typical. We don't tend to be nine-to-fivers. At least I don't. At our house, hours vary with activity, but, on the whole, no one will ever accuse us of being bright-eyed, bushy-tailed morning people.

Climbing onto a plane and winging halfway around the world is a great human equalizer, though. Suddenly we're *all* morning people, evening people, or middle-of-the-night people depending on where the hands of our confused internal clocks are stuck. I usually combat Father Time's cruel travel torture with the modern wonder of a sleeping pill. I'm not sure it helps a whole lot, but at least I store up some needed, very fuzzy shut-eye.

I remember one flight when a large, hairy, and very agitated woman felt it her duty to kick the back of my chair for thirteen hours straight. I haven't seen that kind of stamina outside an IRONMAN race. No amount of reason, pleading, or calling of flight attendants would make her stop. No problem. I figured I'd just take an extra Ambien or two. My wife tells me we had a layover in Paris. All I have is a vague recollection of a cotton-candy dream where everyone spoke French. Not my finest hour.

I'm sure there are scientific reasons to account for all this jet lag, travel, body clock craziness. You know, mathematical equations involving pi and obtuse angles, caffeine, x's and y's, and Greenwich Mean Time. I'm also sure I have no idea what those scientific reasons might be. I *do* know my friend Ben and I found ourselves wide awake at three in the morning on the veranda of a crusty beachside hostel in Tel Aviv listening to waves crash out in the darkness. We were both hungry, but nothing would be open for hours. We decided to drive north.

We roused the sleepy guy in the parking lot kiosk, and he unlocked the gate. Too early for the usual Tel Aviv morning gridlock. Roads wide open. Zigzagging the inevitable Israel metropolitan maze, we made good time getting out of the city. We headed up Highway 6, eventually connecting to 77, and dropped into Tiberias.

Tel Aviv to Tiberias is only about ninety miles—140 kilometers for you metric types—which meant it was still dark when we arrived. At least another hour or two before anything opened. We parked down by the waterfront and walked the boardwalk awhile. Across the lake a cloudless glow on the eastern skyline promised a nice day. When the sun finally crested the Golan Heights, it scattered diamonds across the surface of the Galilee.

Up a side street a man pulled chairs off tables in front of a small café. Still early and not quite time to open, he invited us in anyway. He called to his wife in the kitchen, and she made us a nice Israeli breakfast.

Back in the car, we drove farther north.

Three years of Jesus's adult ministry are recorded in the New

Testament. Most of that time He spent in the region of Galilee. I don't blame Him. It's a wonderful place to wander and reflect. Fields, orchards, forests, streams, waterfalls. Then there's the nearly perfect Mediterranean weather. An altogether beautiful place, top to bottom. Above the Sea of Galilee itself, Highway 90 cuts the western edge of the Hula Valley—part of the larger Syrian-African Rift Valley. The legendary, blood-soaked Golan Heights rise to the east, and the Naftali Mountain Range, to the west. History is everywhere.

I liked traveling with Ben very much. He's read a lot of books by dead men who wrote during a time when the human race relied more on brainpower than Google, and I found his conversation stimulating and fascinating. I found his thoughts on Israel especially intriguing.

He said, "The thing is—and it's especially true in Jerusalem—people become so enamored with the fact they're in Israel that it borders on idolatry."

This was something I'd often thought but never heard voiced in Christian circles.

We continued driving and, thirty-five kilometers or so north of the Sea of Galilee on Highway 90, we came to the town of Qiryat Shemona. Highway 99, the route to Caesarea Philippi, branches east here. You have to watch closely to find it.

We were *not* watching closely.

It didn't take long to realize we'd gone too far. Oh well, a new road to explore. Neither of us felt like turning back.

We drove on up 90 toward Lebanon. The beautiful little border town of Metula lazed in the morning sun. Home of Beit Canada, Israel's only ice-skating rink. Metula has even sent a few athletic hopefuls to the Winter Olympics over the years. Leave it to Israel.

Peach and plum orchards bloomed white and pink around us. I remember thinking, *If I take my first breath in heaven and it looks like Metula, I won't be disappointed.*

The morning stretched its arms, warm and bright. No sound except the bees buzzing the trees. Hard to imagine, in all that peace, the hundreds of terrorist bombings and gunfire attacks that scar the history of this place.

We'd bumped into Lebanon and couldn't go any farther, so we flipped around and found the turn we'd missed. We hiked and explored the rest of the morning and into the afternoon before heading south again toward Tiberias. We were eager to make one more stop that day. A mutual friend, Dr. Dan Stolebarger, had clued us in about a brand-new dig as a don't-miss destination, so we headed toward it, the site of a first-century synagogue on Galilee's shore in the lakeside town of Migdal. I have a lot of respect for Dan. He's an expert scholar and expert on all things Israel. Talk to him for five minutes, and you'll see that passion for the land and people are in his DNA. We figured if Dan said don't miss it, we'd better not miss it.

Except we couldn't find it.

Migdal (*Magdala* in Bible times and the traditional birthplace of Mary Magdalene) is not a large place. So how hard could finding a major excavation be, right?

Well, pretty hard. For us.

The fact that the 3 a.m. wake-up was beginning to feel like it had happened sometime in the 1980s didn't help. We decided to pull over and call Dan back in the States. We'd keep our man cards in our pockets, but desperate times call for desperate measures.

"Hello?" He answered after a few rings.

I explained the problem.

"Where are you?" he said.

"Parked on the side of the road in Migdal."

"Wait! You're in Israel?"

"Pretty sure on that count."

"What do you see around you?"

"Mmm, a roundabout and a gas station. Kind of a mall thing to our left with a grocery store maybe?"

"You have to be kidding me. Keep looking over to your left," Dan said.

We did.

He could have been anywhere on the planet, but Dan came strolling out of a little café in the strip mall and waved us over.

Miracle? Coincidence? Call it what you will, but over the years in that country, I've watched those happy little moments fall out of the sky like apples off a tree. I've even gotten somewhat used to them.

Dan had friends in the café and couldn't leave them, but he gave us directions to the dig. As it turned out, we were practically there already. A little road skirted behind Dan's restaurant and grocery store. Then a hundred yards or so farther on, we found the place. No parking lot, so we pulled onto the grass and dirt across the street from the dig and walked over.

A few college-aged, dust-covered workers lounged in the shade under a wide tarpaulin attached to a wooden shack. One of them introduced herself and offered to show us around.

Gloria was a young archaeologist on loan to the project from a university in Central America. As we walked, she told us the history of the dig.

Father Juan Solana, a Mexican Catholic priest, had long had

a vision for a Christian retreat center in Migdal honoring Mary Magdalene, the close companion of Jesus. By the summer of 2009, he'd raised $20 million, purchased the waterfront parcels, obtained building permits, and even had the cornerstone blessed by the Pope himself. The location was perfect. A stone's throw from Kibbutz Ginosar, home of the Jesus Boat, and just down the road from the Evangelical Triangle, the Bible towns of Capernaum, Bethsaida, and Chorazin. God seemed to smile on Father Juan's plan, and life looked good. The only thing left was the obligatory salvage excavation performed by the Israeli government on all new construction sites.

The Israeli team arrived, and what Father Juan expected to be a quick process slowed down—way down—due to a sticky little piece of red tape. For a month archaeologists poked and prodded every inch of the property. Feeling his timetable and budget slipping through his fingers, Father Juan grew less than happy. Still, the salvage excavation was almost over.

Then, just as the team was about to wrap up, came the "bad" news: they'd found something. Their shovels and picks had struck the top of a wall. The archaeologists gophered on down and turned up a few stone benches. Stunned, excited, unbelieving, they dug farther. There, on the site of the historic Magdala, they uncovered an intact, early first-century synagogue—the only one of its kind ever found in the Galilean villages despite decades of dedicated searching.

The early first century is the exact historical period a young revolutionary named Jesus wandered the area proclaiming a radical new message. Not the message of law or of taking up arms to fight against political tyranny, but a gospel of love and redemption. The book of Matthew tells us that Jesus "went about *all* the cities and villages, teaching in their synagogues, and preaching the gospel of the kingdom, and healing every sickness and every disease among the people" (Matthew 9:35). *All*—this one little word makes the Migdal dig a spectacular historical find.

As she told us the story, I could sense Gloria's pride and excitement. I sensed the treasure she uncovered there in that dusty field wasn't stone or shards of pottery, but faith. I know because I know God. His love is unchanging and unwavering. His love *insists*. Just like it did when Mary Magdalene's face shone with the same joy of discovery on that exact same piece of dirt over two millennia ago.

What a thought! We were standing at the beginning. The very crossroads where the Jewish and Christian faith collided. And here, Gloria told us in her broken English, her faith grew with every spadeful of earth she moved. Uncovering not only dry ruins of stone, but the living story of Love and Grace. Each day and each layer, another chapter. God reaching down to men through His only Son.

Ben and I stood looking at the worn stones beneath our feet. Jesus had stood here. Jesus had taught here. Jesus had breathed here, loved here. And, judging by the light and joy in our new friend's eyes, His story was far from over. In fact, as far as Gloria was concerned it obviously was just beginning.

I love the unrelenting press of history in the Scripture. I love the fact its accuracy is proven time and time again through science and archaeology. Nowhere on earth is this more evident than in Israel.

But I love even more the continuing story still being written in the hearts of men and women every second of every day.

Gloria's joy and faith touched me. I saw in her story the beautiful truth that our God determines to meet each and every one of us somewhere, somehow. Stripping away the labels and designations assigned by man. Catholic, Protestant, Jew, Arab. . . . He presses past our masks, deep into our hearts, planting, watering, drawing, convicting, loving. Desiring nothing but to pull us out of ourselves—out of our carefully constructed boxes, out of the darkness of this world—and into the everlasting light of communion with Him.

Ben and I paused in the cool shade of the ruins. Wind rustled the reeds along the lakeshore, bringing with it snatches of singing from a tour boat out on the water.

> *Could we with ink the ocean fill*
> *And were the skies of parchment made*
> *Were every stalk on earth a quill*
> *And every man a scribe by trade*
> *To write the love of God above*
> *Would drain the ocean dry*
> *Nor could the scroll contain the whole*
> *Though stretched from sky to sky.*

FREDERICK MARTIN LEHMAN (1868-1953)

CHAPTER 7

It Only Takes a Spark

Hiking, driving, the visit to the Migdal dig with Ben . . . by evening I could hardly remember our 3 a.m. wake-up, yet my ears buzzed with exhaustion. Still early evening, but back in our Tiberias hotel room, we collapsed onto our beds.

My phone rang. Dan Stolebarger.

It was Friday, which meant Shabbat—the Jewish Sabbath rest—started just before sundown. That would be any minute now. It would continue through Saturday evening or, officially, until Saturday when the first three stars appear in the sky. Dan wanted us to drive back to Migdal and up the hill to a place called Beit Bracha for a Shabbat gathering. Half dead, I mumbled something I hoped sounded polite but noncommittal. I explained the conversation to Ben. All I got in response was a tired groan from his side of the room.

Five minutes or so passed. I thought Ben had fallen asleep. But then he said, "A Shabbat service?"

"I guess."

Another minute. "You want to go?"

"No way. I'm one hundred percent wiped out. Why? Do you?"

"Nope. I'm not moving."

Traffic noise rumbled several floors below. A horn honked. A couple's muted argument seeped through the wall from the next room. Another few minutes passed.

"Which means we're probably *supposed* to go, right?" Ben said.

Stinking Ben! I sighed. "Yeah, probably."

He stood and stretched.

Seriously? Were we really doing this? My body fighting tooth and nail, I willed myself up off the bed. We got cleaned up, locked the room, and headed out. In the hallway we pushed the button for the elevator.

Nothing happened.

Right. Shabbat. According to Jewish law, Jews are forbidden to do any form of work on the Sabbath. This includes creating a spark or flame. Apparently, with the invention of electricity, pushing buttons or flipping switches fell into this category. And guess what? Elevators have buttons.

Someone please just hit me in the head with a bat.

Some buildings in Israel have Shabbat elevators—superfast rocket ships of happiness that bypass the button-pushing-spark issue by stopping at—that's right—every . . . single . . . floor. Other buildings stop service altogether. Our hotel's brochure advertised itself as a "picturesque 1960s renovated white stucco building with the colorful fixtures of yesteryear." The kind of place I usually look for, but, man, I was tired to my bones. All I wanted was my bed. And if I couldn't have that, I at least wanted an elevator.

I got stairs instead. I'm pretty sure I heard angels laughing—*at* me, not *with* me.

"At least it's downhill," Ben said.

"We still have to come back up."

Tiberias up to Migdal only took ten minutes or so. I spent the drive time praying that the Shabbat gathering (I'd never been to one) would involve copious amounts of coffee. We followed the directions Dan gave and turned into a quaint, local neighborhood nestled against the base of Mount Arbel. Not what I'd expected. As we wound up the hill, we passed houses, a school, a small store, a café, more houses. A skinny dog ran alongside us for a block or so, challenging us who were strangers on his turf. At length, we pulled into a narrow gravel parking area across the street from a couple buildings that appeared to be a residence. Potted shrubs, palms, plants. The smell of flowers laced the air as evening fell. A red tile roof and clean stucco walls. A pretty place. We knocked on the thick double doors. They opened, and Dan smiled at us as he ushered us into a long common area.

I immediately smelled coffee. *Hallelujah!*

Doors to a few guest rooms lined each side of the long room. Dan led us out through a sliding glass door onto a wide, flagstone veranda overlooking the lights of Migdal and the Sea of Galilee beyond.

We talked awhile, Dan telling us a little about Beit Bracha, a Christian retreat center operating under the umbrella of CMJ Israel, an organization going back to the 1830s and dedicated to teaching Gentiles about Christianity's Jewish roots and promoting spiritual restoration among the Jews. In other words, encouraging their recognition of Jesus as Messiah.

Dan and his wife, Sharon, had led nearly thirty tours to Israel and seen a lot. I always love a chance to pick his brain.

"So, Dan, you're a veteran Israel traveler. What's the most impactful moment in Israel you can remember?"

"Oh, man," he said. "We've been so many times. There are really too many to mention. But the time I spend on Mount Arbel, when I'm overlooking the Galilee region, is special. I like to think of it as Jesus's school of discipleship up there. But every site in Israel is unique. Each one always provides the perfect backdrop for whatever I'm teaching. I'm telling you, if you listen carefully, the rocks are still crying out. I've also loved working with the young IDFers on the bases."

"I'm jealous of that. I've wanted to visit the bases, but I've never had the open door. What are they like?"

He shook his head. "Dirty. Messy. And it's always a shock to see how young the recruits are. They're curious about why we're there, about why we'd even come. I mean, they're conscripted into service. So they have to wonder why anyone would willingly volunteer, right? But we jump in and work side by side."

"So you win them over."

"Mostly. The thing about Israelis, they're prickly on the outside but soft on the inside. We usually learn again the Hatikvah (the Israeli national anthem). We have a meal and sing it together before we leave. It still amazes me to see tears from both our group and the soldiers."

"Do you stay in touch with any of them?"

"Absolutely. We've become pretty emotionally invested. We've even worked alongside soldiers who've been killed, and their Jewish commanders have sent word to ask us to pray. It's the real deal out there."

Having access to a guy with so much history in the Holy Land, I was curious about his thoughts on the future of the country. "So, what do you see coming for Israel? I know there are so many end-times camps. Where do you pitch your tent these days?"

"'I see a bad moon a-rising, I see trouble on the way.' . . . Sorry, I couldn't help myself," he said. "In a nutshell, we know Jerusalem will be the center of attention, and it'll cause a global hernia, as it says in Zechariah. God's not finished with Israel, and I think believers will play an important part in its spiritual restoration. Whether it's the Psalm 83 scenario or Ezekiel 38 and 39, God is setting up the end-of-days chessboard."

"So you think things are close?"

"Honestly, over the years my thoughts have changed, and I now feel like I have more questions than answers. So when it comes to eschatology . . . I tossed the pen a while back, and now I write in pencil. I also make sure I have a good eraser. That being said, I still believe that we need to be like the tribe of Issachar. They had the reputation of knowing the times and, more importantly, knowing what Israel should do. I think that's one of the main reasons Sharon and I are trying our best to get as many people as possible to come with us to Israel. The future is too important to let anybody else shape your opinion about what God is doing."

I thought about all the spiritual/political lenses today. "It does seem like a lot of opinion shaping is going on out there."

"No doubt. And I find it significant how concerned Israel is these days with the views of the forty-and-under crowd."

"Why do you think that's the case?"

"Because the older generation's view has already been set. So then the important question is this: what is the passion of the generations that are further removed from the Holocaust and the miracle of the birth of Israel in 1948? But the problem is, it's expensive to come to Israel. So a lot of the younger people don't. They never see for themselves what's really going on. In the end, their views are only influenced by a media that no longer wants to inform but only to shape opinion."

We looked out over the lights. Water trickled in a small pond. Somewhere, someone sang in gentle Hebrew. I felt glad to be there. I also felt that familiar Hand on my shoulder. The still Voice. "*And you didn't want to come . . .*"

"I was tired."

"*I've had this for you . . .*"

As it always does, that old fight in me crumbled and fell away, broken. Gone was the subliminal clash of swords and cannon thunder.

And in the echoes of the silence, peace.

The Beit Bracha Prayer and Retreat Center. *Beit Bracha*: "House of Blessing." Let me tell you, through the years of travel and in many locations and situations, I've come to believe deeply in discernment. A discernment outside of my own brain and emotion. There are places in the world where I've felt such heaviness of spirit it was almost hard to breathe.

And then there was Beit Bracha.

Half a world away from my own address, I knew I was home.

Beit Bracha is owned and run by followers of Yeshua. Not the usual state of affairs in a country where the Christian population is only about 2 percent. The staff is made up primarily of volunteers, of beautiful, loving people who come from all over the globe and serve the community with joy. What a testimony to the mission of Christ! At this little Galilean outpost of light, everyone who walks through the door is welcomed with deep and sincere love. Ben and I were no exception to that rule. I knew I'd been an idiot to fight coming.

A couple approached, and Dan introduced us to Ted and Linda Walker, our hosts. Originally from the United States, Ted and Linda had been in Israel for decades. Their roots in the land and love for people ran deep, and both were evident in everything they did and said. They welcomed us warmly and invited us over into a separate building. A large, open living room, dining room, and kitchen area.

Guests trickled in, faces red from heat and sun and a day spent exploring paths of Christ and kings. Several different languages colored the conversation. Once we all were seated, Ted prayed, deep and heartfelt. We sang something everyone seemed to know except me. It didn't matter. We broke bread together: we *communed*. The room warmed as did the mood. Laughter, talk, fellowship due to our common bond of Jesus. A bond that accepts no borders, be they barbed wire, brick, or stained glass. A bond that can't be severed by differences in culture, language, or color of skin. I'd been to a lot of cross-topped buildings over the years, but here, I realized, is *church*.

Ted stood and read from the Bible. What a surreal joy to hear Scripture, to gather in the love and fellowship of Jesus in the land He loved, not two miles away from a place where He had taught. I felt so thankful not to have missed any of this evening.

When Ted finished reading, he invited a young couple up. The young man seated himself on a folding chair and began to pick out a melody on an old Spanish guitar. His wife, eyes closed, sang a worship song in soft Hebrew. Just the two of them. No $100,000 sound system or light show. No studio magic or pitch correction. To this day I don't think I've ever heard anything so beautiful.

I'm not usually a crier. But as people around me joined in the song, having been led to the throne of God by this humble, unassuming couple, I bowed my head and, through blurry eyes, watched my tears fall to the floor. . . .

Now, I believe in miracles because I've seen too many to deny that God does the impossible. I know my God. And I know He set appointments for us even before He laid the foundations of the earth. And I knew that, sitting in that place, with those people, a new family—most of whom I didn't even know—I'd crashed headlong into one of those appointments. Maybe it started with Dan walking out of that restaurant. What were the odds? And the fact we "just happened" to cross paths as Shabbat started. I'd almost been derailed by fatigue and devils, but, pulled along by Ben's obedience and the Spirit of Life, up the hill I went to be held close by Love.

For a long time afterward, we sat and talked with Dan and Ted and Linda, our new old friends. Later that night, I was finally in bed. Tired as I was, I lay awake for a long time, held by Goodness—another familiar and wonderful feeling. Crushed, torn, rebuilt. I thought about how badly, even as we had knocked on Beit Bracha's thick doors, I had wanted to climb back in the car, return to the hotel, and sleep. Our flesh, spurred on by the prince of this world, can be a powerful force. But he's no match—not even close—for the Father. The Almighty Himself had insisted on my attending this meeting, and He graced me with one of the most deeply moving spiritual experiences of my life.

There on that thin mattress, five stories above the dirt on which God's Son had led His earthly life, He breathed *good night* to my tired soul.

And I felt like I had been born again . . . again.

CHAPTER 8

Elvis and the Hebrew Word for Diesel

Although I've had my share of critics, I like to think I have a fairly good handle on the English language. On a good day, I might even be able to make myself understood in broken Spanish. Sort of. At least enough to ask where the bathroom is and order black coffee. Obviously not in that order.

But Hebrew is an interesting animal. Written right to left, spoken in every direction imaginable, it jangles, pops, and growls. It's a good language. A language that carries its own weight. In my opinion, a tongue birthed expressly to communicate all the passion, joy, and pain of this human existence.

It's also a language that makes it practically impossible for a wandering American songwriter like me to get gasoline.

Every good tourist, no matter the destination, does his best to collect three or four good local words. Travelers to Israel are no exception. We easily remember *boker tov*—"good morning"—because, as the tour guide points out, it sounds a lot like *broken toe*. Thus, the day after arrival, a lot of *broken toes* fly around the Israeli hotel breakfast halls. *Toda*—"thank you"—is another polite favorite, very useful after gift-shop purchases or to say to the McDonald's countergirl who reminds you, no, you *can't* have cheese on your hamburger. *Toda* is easy too. Just add an *a* on the end of *toad*.

Then there's the big one. You already know it. *Shalom.* Shalom is the granddaddy Holy Land–tourist word of them all. We pack it in our brains around the same time we squeeze extra socks and underwear into our carry-ons. And, brother, as soon as we hit the ground at Ben Gurion, everybody is fair game.

Of course the first Israeli we meet is the customs agent.

"Shalom!" we say. We're a little anxious, so this first linguistic toe dip happens about three feet before we actually arrive at the window.

The agent doesn't bite. Just looks over our passports with the same bored disdain taught at Custom Agent Schools around the globe. After just enough time to get our hearts racing with the thought we might actually get spanked, spun, and turned away, he grunts, stamps, and reluctantly grants us entrance. We're relieved and humbled by this great show of benevolence. "Shalom," we say again (we haven't learned *toda* yet), but he's already beckoning the next bright-eyed pilgrim forward.

We're nothing if not persistent. A few minutes later, in the airport itself, we're happy to find our greetings often returned. Money changers, rental-car clerks, SIM-card swappers—all of them shalom us right back. And so it should be.

Shalom is the Hebrew word for peace. And the one thing most longed for on that little chunk of geography is shalom. Here is a place that's known war, or the threat of war, for much of its inhabited existence. In the Old Testament, specifically Isaiah 9:6, the prophet referenced the coming Messiah with the name *Sar Shalom*—the Prince of

Peace. Peace, wholeness, health, welfare, safety, tranquility, prosperity, perfectness, fullness, rest—*shalom* speaks to the reality God longs for us to know. In fact, the word *shalom* reveals the very heart of God.

And God, whether we choose to recognize it or not, is at the very heart of Israel. So, for me, watching the bread vendor next to the Jaffa Gate getting bombarded by fifty *shaloms* from fifty happy, footsore tourists isn't a bad thing. The genuine smile on his face tells me he agrees. I'm sure a few shekels in his pocket and five or ten rings of his sesame bread and hyssop being passed around the group didn't hurt either.

Shalom. A great word. An *important* word.

But *shalom* wasn't the word I scoured my fatigued brain for one morning when I woke before the sun to gas up the van. No, what I needed at that moment was the Hebrew word for *diesel*. But I couldn't find it. Oh well, I figured it would hit me on the way to the station. Still half asleep, I climbed in and turned on the engine. While the motor warmed, rattling the morning stillness, I opened the GPS app on my phone. *Thank You, Jesus, for GPS.*

Israel is a very wired country, and the Waze app is brilliant. Although now popular in the United States, Waze was developed by an Israli company. It offers real-time driving information provided by real users, 24/7. Plus, at the time of this trip, it offered an optional Elvis voice to give me directions. I couldn't resist that one. You haven't lived until you've been guided through the Holy Land by Semitic Elvis. Let me say, the Jewish people have given the world much of history's great innovations. Einstein's Theory of Relativity casts a long shadow. Vaccines for cholera, the bubonic plague, and polio are nice to have around. Modern Israel gave us thumb drives, drip irrigation, and cherry tomatoes. But when you're travel-dazed, sleep-deprived, and a little lost, having Elvis ride shotgun with you is the stuff of dreams.

Off we went.

"Uh, turn left, baby," the King said.

I did.

Winding down a steep hill, I offered a prayer to heaven for an open gas station.

"Hey, Priscilla, turn right at the roundabout, baby," the King instructed.

Cool, Elvis. Will do, but don't call me "Priscilla."

Tiberias, a town nestled into the hills on the western shore of the Sea of Galilee. Founded by Herod Antipas under Roman rule during Jesus's lifetime; named after the emperor Tiberias. Like most communities here, probably built on ruins even more ancient. Through the millennia the city has survived earthquakes and wars as well as Roman, Arabic, and Jewish control. There are still buildings marked with holes from bullets that flew in from across the Sea of Galilee during the war of Yom Kippur. This is a back-and-forth, up-and-down kind of place where nothing happens in a straight line. Especially the roads.

"Turn left. Turn right. Turn left. Make a U-turn, baby." Elvis didn't sound at all confident.

A couple roundabouts later I thanked God for a lighted sign above a petrol station. I pulled in. Waking before the roosters meant I was the only car at the place. *Good.* I knew I needed all the time I could get. I didn't want impatient taxi drivers or overland truckers honking at me to hurry. I stared at the Hebrew letters on the pump for a while like maybe if I waited long enough, the words would flip left to right and morph to English. There was a slot for my credit card, but that was one rabbit hole I wasn't willing to go down. Not when I couldn't read the writing. No choice left to me, I headed for the little gas-station market.

Music played as I walked in. That familiar droning soundtrack of the Middle East. No customers. Just a couple of guys behind a counter. I did one more quick mental search for the word for *diesel* but came up with *nada*.

Good tourist that I was, I fished out the next best thing. "Shalom."

A young guy in a white t-shirt and brown polyester pants leaned on the counter next to the register. He looked me up and down but said nothing.

I tried again. "Shalom."

He shrugged and kind of sang the reply, a little sarcasm around the edge. "Sha-lom."

His buddy, heavier, in greasy, blue coveralls, said, "*Salaam alaikum*." Clearly meant as a correction to an ignorant Western tourist. *Salaam alaikum*, Arabic, but basically the same meaning.

"*Alaikum salaam*"—meaning "Peace be upon you also"—was my response.

"You speak Arabic?" Coveralls said.

"Nope. That's it. I'm tapped out. You speak English?"

The young, thin one shook his head and rattled something off. Whether Hebrew or Arabic, I had no idea. I'm a musician—and it was early in the morning. I struggled for the word for *diesel* again.

"Nah, I'm kidding," Thin Guy said. "I speak English."

Thank You, Jesus. I wanted to hug the guy. "Good! Man, I'm trying to get diesel, but I can't read the Hebrew on the pump."

Coveralls started for the door. "Don't worry. I'll fill it for you. You pay him after."

"Thanks," I said.

When Coveralls had gone, Thin Guy ran his fingers through his hair. "You are American?"

I said I was.

"I love America," he said.

"Why?"

"Because there is opportunity in America. There is hope in America."

"There isn't opportunity in Israel?"

"Not for me. I only have the opportunity to work in a petrol station."

I felt ignorant about this.

"So come visit America," I said.

"I cannot get a visa. I'm Palestinian."

"Aah. . . . Are you Muslim?"

"A little."

"You can be Muslim a *little*?"

He shrugged. "Sometimes you can. You want coffee?"

Now I really did want to give him a hug. I told him so. This is apparently not funny in the Palestinian-little-bit-Muslim world. He pointed to a pot on a warmer.

"You are Jewish? You don't look Jewish," he said.

"No, I'm Christian."

"A little bit Christian?"

"The whole bit." I watched his reaction. Not much to speak of.

"You don't mind that I'm Christian?" I asked.

He lifted a shoulder. "You are what you are. You want me to be Christian?"

I sipped coffee. "Of course. There's hope in Christianity whether you're in America or Israel. Do you want to be?"

He shook his head. "I can't be Christian. I'm Muslim."

"But only a little bit."

"It only takes a little bit. But I wish I could come to America."

"So do I." I really did too. I liked the kid, and I wanted him to have hope. "I'd buy you coffee."

"You have good coffee in America? Arabic coffee?"

"No, we have Starbucks."

He pointed to the pot on the warmer. "But better than this?"

I went the diplomatic route. "Any coffee's good right now."

I'm sure he knew it was a dodge, but he didn't say anything.

Coveralls came back in. My little-bit-Muslim guy rang me up and ran my credit card. Then he pointed at Coveralls. "He is Muslim."

"A little bit?" I said.

"No, all of him."

"I'm Christian," I said to Coveralls.

"Okay," he said and lit a cigarette.

My new friend handed me my card back.

"*Toda*," I said.

"Welcome," he said.

For some reason I couldn't explain, at that moment I felt sorry I had to leave. I reached out a hand, and he took it.

"*Salaam*. Peace. I pray you find it," I said.

"Shalom," he said.

At the door I turned. "Hey, how do you say *diesel* in Hebrew?"

The young man smiled. "Same as in Arabic: *diesel.*"

CHAPTER 9

Bones

I'd done a short tour with Randy Stonehill before. I'd met him briefly a couple times. But I really got to know him when we traveled through Greece, Turkey, and Israel with a couple of his fellow contemporary Christian music (CCM) legends, Phil Keaggy and Bob Bennett. After the trip, the four of us collaborated on a recording project. What a blessing to work with some of my early songwriting heroes. Randy and I especially connected musically. We went on to write and make a couple Stonehill and Storm records and tour together as schedules allowed.

I like writing songs with Randy. He's brilliant, quick, and keeps me on my toes. He makes me laugh. He's also not afraid to tell me when something isn't my best work. I like to think we push each other. I'm proud of the music we've made as a result.

"You got anything?" he asked me one day as we looked at each other over our guitars.

"I don't know. Maybe. Kind of a loose idea based on Ezekiel's valley of dry bones."

Randy opened a Bible and read the passage, spending a few

minutes soaking in the poetry of it. I played him a bit and sang a verse
I'd been banging around. A dark, minor-key, Dylanesque groove.

In a valley of dust off of Highway 10
The fingers of God are stirring the wind
The heavenly dance is about to begin
Bones
Borders of countries and borders of men
Cities of angels and cities of sin
Covered with blood and with muscle and skin
Bones

We traded lines for a couple hours. When we finished, we both
smiled. A good day's work.

Bones. . . .

Several years earlier, before I had ever set foot in the Middle East,
I was on the Caribbean coast of Honduras when I met a travel-worn
guy sitting next to a backpack on the wooden steps of a little shanty-
town market. This wasn't the sort of place you ran into another white
guy. Curious to hear his story, I walked over and shook his hand.
He introduced himself as Samuel and invited me to sit. As we gazed
out over the turquoise water, he told me in heavily accented English
he was a Jew, Israeli born and raised. Recently out of the IDF, he'd
wanted to see some of the world, so he decided to take a hike, starting
in South America and heading north.

"That's a crazy long hike, man," I said.

"It's not bad." He said it like he'd just walked around the block.

"So you've come all the way to Central America. How far will
you go?" I said.

He scratched his beard. "Guatemala next. Then up through Mexico, I think."

I told him I'd been to Mexico, and I'd always wanted to see Israel. I told him my grandfather had been there.

He nodded. "Israel is a miracle. Like God told the prophet Ezekiel."

"You know the Old Testament. Are you religious?" I asked.

He said he wasn't, particularly, but like many Jewish boys, he'd studied the Torah when he was young.

We talked for a while. An interesting guy. After a bit he stood and hoisted his pack. We shook hands, said our goodbyes, and he headed north up the beach, boots throwing sand up behind him.

Later that night I sat beneath a flickering light bulb on the front porch of a stilted bungalow listening to O. Henry's "Banana Republic" rain beat a tattoo on the tin roof, air scented with ocean and wet earth. A tiny spider hung in the mouth of a beer bottle on a wicker table next to an ashtray full of somebody's old cigarette butts. Who knew how long they'd been there? Time moved slowly in that part of the world. I picked up my guitar and started strumming a John Prine song.

"A miracle," Samuel had said. Had he found a place out of the rain? It fell harder, and my mind turned to God. I thanked Him for the night and the smell of the sea.

Make me an angel, that flies from Montgomery. . . .

When I thought about it, Samuel was right. There was no reasonable explanation for the presence of Israel as a nation on the world stage, yet there it was. Defined borders, its own currency, Hebrew as the national language. . . .

O. Henry, one of my favorite writers, used the Honduran coast as the location for several of his short stories. But in his day—he died in 1910—it would have been impossible to happen across a young Israeli on the beach. More than impossible save for a few fringe theologians clinging to the outmoded idea that Old Testament prophecy regarding Israel was still legitimate. Most Western Christians operated under the assumption that the church had replaced Israel in God's eyes. A *real* Israel? The world would have laughed at the thought. After all, the Jews as a people had been scattered all over the globe a couple thousand years ago. There would *never* be a national Israel again.

Except for one thing. God had said it would happen.

So it happened.

Make me a poster of an old rodeo. . . .

The rain came harder.

Standing on top of the Mount of Olives, my wife, Michelle, and I looked down over the Jewish cemetery across the Kidron Valley. Our vantage point offered a stunning view of the Temple Mount: the gold-topped Dome of the Rock—standing next to the Al Aqsa Mosque—brilliantly reflected the sunlight. Below the buildings the outline of the Eastern (Golden) Gate, filled in and walled with stone, stood sentinel over a Muslim graveyard. Both the walled-in gate and the boneyard were Islamic insurance against the expected return and entry into the Old City of the Jewish Messiah prophesied in Ezekiel 44.

Definitely a surreal spot to visit. The New Testament tells us Jesus ascended from somewhere close to the place we stood. And to the Mount of Olives He is promised to return: "And in that day His feet will stand on the Mount of Olives, which faces Jerusalem on the east. And the Mount of Olives shall be split in two, from east to west" (Zechariah 14:4). Christians believe this prophecy refers to the second coming—the promised return of Jesus—whereas Jews see it simply as the longed-for appearance of their messiah.

Then, from the mount—Christians and Jews agree on the how, if not the who—He'll descend into the valley, enter through the Golden Gate, and take His place on the Temple Mount to rule the nations.

If God speaks universes into existence, I doubt a handful of stones and bones will keep Him out.

Below, on our side of the valley, a group of black-clad mourners gathered around a stone-topped grave. The cemetery that spreads across those slopes is the largest and holiest Jewish burial ground in the world, started during the First Temple period—three thousand years ago—and still used today. More than seventy thousand graves. Some of the most celebrated and important figures in Judaism are buried there. And Jewish tradition promises those buried on the Mount of Olives will be the first to experience resurrection.

Michelle and I walked down the mountain along a narrow lane bordered by high stone walls. The road leveled as we neared the bottom. We stepped through a doorway into the biblical Garden of Gethsemane. The group we were with gathered into a tight bunch as our tour guide shared the storied history of the place. Michelle and I drifted off on our own to take a look around. Not hard to imagine that dark night of prayerful agony while Roman torches wound down the hill from the city.

Walking along the back of the garden, we noticed a hole a few feet deep sunk next to the stone wall. Curious, we stepped down into it. At the bottom, a low metal grate was mortared into the stone. Behind it, a pile of bones, a few human skulls among them.

Over the years I've asked people—scholars, locals, tour guides—about those bones. Everyone can tell me the olive trees there are over two thousand years old, dating to Jesus's time. They can show me the grotto where the disciples slept through prayer time. They know all about the tomb where tradition claims Mary, the mother of Jesus, is buried. But about those bones they just shrug. After all, who really cares? What's one more pile of bones in a land with nearly four thousand years of recorded history? "This place is *built* on bones. It's *all* bones," they say.

But they weren't just bones to me. For some reason they lodged themselves in my soul, in my imagination. The thought fascinated me: here were bones that once gave shape to living beings. Beings with thoughts and creativity and songs. Somebody loved them. Maybe they had enemies. They worked and played. What did they dream about when they slept? They knew suffering, heartache, and joy. They all felt the sun on their backs and the wind on their faces.

They ate, drank, loved. They lived life.

They were people just like Michelle and me.

Just like Ezekiel, Samuel the hiker, John Prine, and O. Henry.

Michelle and I always look for those bones when we visit the garden. As morbid as it seems, I find them hopeful. Among those tens of thousands of graves and shrines—all shapes and sizes, every one a reminder of our mortality—I remember what Samuel said on that Caribbean beach: *Israel is a miracle.*

Because, when it comes down to it, God is not in the business of death. He is the Giver of life. He's the breath of Adam, and He's an empty tomb. He is joy and light and eternity.

Israel is impossible. An indisputable miracle on the modern stage. And Israel exists because God promised it would. I love that fact. I think of it every time I stand onstage and sing about Ezekiel's dry bones. If God could work this miracle of Israel against all worldly odds and dark spiritual forces, there is one thing I can take to the bank: His promises are true; they will not be denied.

And God promises me He will never leave me nor forsake me.

He promises to complete the work He began in me.

He promises that one day He and I will walk arm in arm through the canyons of eternity. And when the stars fade around us, suns burn out, the galaxies are nothing but a distant memory, hosts of angels will sing His praises still. He will still love me, and I will still love Him.

And, bones forgotten, our story will just be getting started.

CHAPTER 10

The Garden

I have tarried in the Garden
I've rested in the sound of Spanish hymns
Filled with the mystery of pardon
And the wondering of grace bestowed to men.

MY SONG "THE GARDEN"

Many of the stories and encounters in this book are of the off-the-beaten-path variety. But God is not limited. At times He takes us to the mat with the weight of His grace and love smack-dab in the middle of the *beaten* path.

The first invitation my wife, Michelle, and I received to travel to Israel came at a tough time. We lived in northern Idaho, and almost fifteen hundred miles south in Yuma, Arizona, my stepdad was in the last weeks of his life, fighting advanced cancer. I held the Israel trip loosely, knowing I'd need to be there for my mom when the time came.

Just days before the Israel flight, I got the call. His body was failing; this was it. I hopped a southbound plane. It's never easy watching someone pass. Jerry had been a big man. A strong man. Not the shell I saw on that hospital bed temporarily in the living room. He hadn't signed over his life-deed to Jesus till the last year or two, but he'd always been a person of character. Kind, giving, simple, and unwavering in his convictions. He'd worked hard as a tractor mechanic all his life.

Jerry came into my life in my early teen years. At a time when life had knocked me down and kicked me in the ribs with steel-toed boots. I was young, broken, drifting. Trying to find my feet. Jerry was strong, firm of hand, and singular of voice. Suffice to say, we did not often see eye to eye.

Years later, as the proud genius of my youth dulled, I came to appreciate that steady presence. Even more so as my own children came along.

I'll never forget the moment tough, steady Jerry Beard stepped into the next world. It was as if he'd planned it. On the radio in the corner, Fernando Ortega sang, "And when I've come to die, give me Jesus." Such quiet dignity. Such peace. Such grace.

But no time to grieve for me. I caught a flight home and grabbed my guitar. Straight back to the airport.

Next stop, Tel Aviv.

The bus tour moved like a whirlwind. So much to see, so much to absorb. I thought about Jerry but shoved the emotion to the back of my heart. *Later*, I told myself. *Deal with it later.*

Jerusalem proved loud, busy, fast-paced. We rushed from site to site. The Western Wall, Garden of Gethsemane, the Mount of Olives—I lost track. Then, late one afternoon, the bus stopped on a narrow street outside the Old City's Damascus Gate in a rough-looking Muslim neighborhood. We filed off, a glassy-eyed horde, and shuffled up a narrow alley and through a doorway in the stone wall. . . .

The beautiful oasis of the Garden Tomb.

Now, some people are familiar with the hymn "It Is Well with My Soul," written by Horatio Spafford after the tragic and traumatic loss of his daughters at sea. Fewer are familiar with the fact he and his wife, Anna, still reeling with the emotion of the loss, went on to settle in Jerusalem and founded the American Colony in the Old City. The idea was simple: Christians living in book-of-Acts-like community, sharing and having all things in common. They opened their doors to Arabs, Jews, and Bedouins alike, seeking to live out their faith. Today the place still stands as the American Colony Hotel. Hanging in the lobby are Spafford's original, handwritten lyrics to his hymn that's touched and given hope to so many people.

In 1892 well-known British leader General Charles Gordon settled in Palestine. He often visited the Spaffords. One time when he was staying with them, he looked out from his window above the Old City wall and spotted a rocky hill with what he determined to be the distinct features of a skull. An intrepid explorer and naturally curious, he investigated. What he discovered was an ancient tomb that had all the historical earmarks of the property of Joseph of Arimathea, the wealthy man Scripture tells us took responsibility for the removal and burial of Jesus's body after His crucifixion.

Gordon was excited, as were many others. In the third century Constantine's mother had picked the Church of the Holy Sepulchre as the scene of Jesus's death and resurrection, and centuries of tradition had supported her claim. Yet now, in the late nineteenth century, many were convinced that General Gordon's theory made more sense scripturally and archaeologically. Back in London a group of

Christians raised funds and purchased the area around the tomb, and the Garden Tomb Association was born. This entity still owns the property to this day.

Yet endless material exists—pros and cons—regarding the historical significance of this place. My purpose here isn't to add to that collection. Frankly, to me, the event is much more important than the location. In the risen Christ I put my faith. I *will* say the detail at the Garden Tomb site, taken side by side with Scripture, is extremely compelling.

Stepping through the gate, I was immediately struck by the cool quiet of the place after the loud bus and the hot grime of the street. An elderly, white-bearded man greeted us with a thick Scottish brogue. He explained he'd be our guide and would answer any questions we might have. He chatted some details as we strolled through the cool greenery. At the back of the garden, he paused to show us Golgotha itself. The eye sockets and nose of the skull stood out clearly in the low afternoon sun. Below, diesel engines rattled and horns honked— the soundscape of a busy bus station.

We moved deeper into the garden. Not a lot of people there that day. A small group in a secluded alcove took communion and sang hymns in Spanish. The tomb itself stood open in the cliff.

We took turns going in, a few at a time.

Our turn came.

We went in.

We looked around the tight space. A slow turn revealed an empty burial shelf. An ancient cross painted on the wall. Hewn stone. Air heavy with age.

We came out.

I searched myself for some deep spiritual experience. I mean, here it was, right? Everything I'd heard, read, and studied, converging at this very place. I dug deep, fished around. Nothing. I felt numb.

When the last travelers were out, we all took seats on stone benches, our Scottish friend in front of us.

"What did you think?" he said.

Several answered. Everyone clearly impacted.

I still really had nothing.

"Can I tell you a story?" he said.

Of course he could. Everyone knows you never refuse a bearded Scot when he offers a story.

In the book of Acts, it is said of Peter and John, fresh from Pentecost, the elders "began to recognize them as having been with Jesus" (Acts 4:13 NASB). I think I saw the same thing in the precious face of that old man that day there in the garden. He smiled, tender and kind. His eyes welled.

Here is a man who has been with Jesus.

Then he began to talk. Simply, perfectly, he gave his testimony. He took his time, no word more important than another. He told us of a wandering young man, filled with himself, scarred and hardened by the world. And he told how the King of the universe reached down and touched him. Drew him. Loved him.

He told his story.

He told my story.

I don't know if his story touched the others. I hope so. Either way, the truth of the matter hung fresh and clear in the still of the afternoon. While the Catholics and Protestants thumb-wrestled and threw lawn darts at each other over archaeological and theological fences, here—in the precious memories and beautiful face of this elderly saint—was the thing that really mattered. Here was

Michelangelo's *Creation of Adam*. Here was God's insistent press to rescue us from ourselves.

Here, not in stone but in the testament of a changed life, was the empty tomb.

I grieved then.

As the others filed away, I grieved. In that quiet place I wept. I wept for the suffering and pain the Son of God took on for my selfishness and pride. For the loss of Jerry, a man whose steady, quiet ways did much to shape my life, though I might not have recognized or appreciated it at the time. I wept for myself, joyous in the fact that—by the grace of God, by the power over death proclaimed both in that empty hole not ten feet away, and in the testimony of God's saints—I would see Jerry again.

And I would see my God face-to-face.

Singing floated across the garden. Spanish words, but I recognized the song anyway.

When peace like a river attendeth my way
When sorrows like sea billows roll
Whatever my lot
Thou hast taught me to say
It is well, it is well with my soul.

And it was.

CHAPTER 11

Same Ol' Sun

The October sun shone warm on the Galilee, a celestial Midas touching the autumn-brown grass on the hills and turning it gold. It was a special trip for Michelle and me, as we were traveling with my mom, sister, mother-in-law, sister-in-law, and nephew as well as several friends. We were excited about showing them off-the-bus Israel. We drove east along Highway 99 close to the northern border and the demilitarized zone. We passed Dan, a picturesque little kibbutz complete with a natural history museum, tiny zoo, and winery. We didn't have time to stop. Past the town we turned left on the narrow, don't-blink-or-you'll-miss-it road leading to the Tel Dan Nature Reserve. We parked next to the store at the trailhead and climbed out.

I love Tel Dan and always look forward to visiting and hiking it. Cool, clear streams rush through the trees and thick undergrowth. Snow and rain from the distant heights of Mount Hermon well up, fresh spring water forming the Dan River and, later, its big brother, the Jordan.

Much like Banias a few miles away, Dan is rich in history.

Plentiful water and fertile farmland have drawn inhabitants to the area for thousands of years. Old Testament writers called the city Laish and described it as a peaceful place, the inhabitants living in safety and security. That is, until the tribe of Dan showed up.

The book of Joshua tells us the sons of Dan conquered the people and renamed the city after their father. The name stands to this day.

Sometime later—but still nearly a thousand years before Christ—Solomon, like his father, David, possessed the wisdom and strength of leadership needed to hold together a tense and fraying nation made up of twelve distinct tribes, each with its own demands and agenda. Solomon had asked God for the wisdom to lead. Good thing he did—for they were strong-willed people. Solomon did well until the end of his reign when he fell to sin, bringing in foreign wives and concubines and setting up places of false worship for them. God was not happy, and He promised to divide the kingdom.

And whenever God promises something, it happens.

When Solomon died in 931 BC, his son Rehoboam stepped into his sandals. Problem was, they were pretty big sandals.

Tired of being stretched see-through thin by Solomon's plethora of building projects, the northern tribes bucked and demanded relief. They got out their bullhorns, made sandwich-board signs, and marched for tax cuts. Rehoboam got nervous. Seems this king deal might have been harder than he'd thought. He sought the counsel of his father's old and trusted advisers. "Go easy on them," they told him. "Calm 'em down and you'll win 'em over." Not exactly what he wanted to hear. Rehoboam apparently went by the old adage *If you don't like what your counselor says, find a new one.* He called in the younger set and posed the same question. His buddies suggested he not only keep the people's feet to the flames, but crank up the heat. The show-'em-who's-boss approach. Sounded good. Rehoboam liked being boss. New blood, new ideas.

He went along with the young guys.

The result? War on a grand scale. . . . Thanks, boys.

Enter Jeroboam.

Now Jeroboam had been one of Solomon's original superintendents. As the revolt against Rehoboam picked up steam, Jeroboam found himself one of the leaders of the rebellion. The herd liked what they saw, and it wasn't long before he was made king of the northern tribes, leaving Rehoboam in the south—and in the dust.

Not a bad setup for Jeroboam. But as time passed he saw that the people of the north hadn't shaken their spiritual ties to Jerusalem and the temple, their ties to Judah. And Judah was in the south, Rehoboam's end of the swimming pool.

Jeroboam put his mind to the problem and came up with an idea. Not a new or especially creative idea, but an idea: he'd undermine the monopoly of ritual worship set up by David and Solomon in Jerusalem and build a couple temples of his own. After all, how hard could it be? He'd put one in Bethel and one in Dan so no one would have to travel too far. Plus, he'd go Jerusalem one better. He'd up the ante by adding a few golden calves to the mix. One more carnival sideshow in the long history of Israel's idol-worship detours.

We talked about these things as we hiked along through the trees next to the water. At a wooden bridge we stepped off the trail to let several young gun-carrying soldiers pass. Then we moved on, cool and shaded along the stream. At length, dark rock walls appeared, indications of ancient habitation. Farther on, stones beneath our feet—

a road. I couldn't help but wonder about the people who had walked those stones smooth, all those thousands of years ago. People with hopes, dreams, loves. People just like our little band of travelers.

We wound our way up the road and out into the courtyard of Jeroboam's temple. As we arrived, a large tour group exited the opposite direction, heading for their bus, and we had the place almost to ourselves. All quiet except for the birds and the soft wind in the trees. A fabricated metal frame depicting the dimensions of Jeroboam's original altar gleamed in the sun. A beautifully evil place. Remnants of human effort, of man distracting fellow man from the truth and love of the living God for selfish gain. Wise Solomon said there was nothing new under the sun. Thinking about a few of the worship centers I'd been to, rich in flash but bankrupt in heavenly intimacy, I figured the old man knew what he was talking about.

The group climbed up and explored the temple. I hung back and watched. This was border country. We practically stood on the 1949 Israeli Syrian Armistice Line edging the demilitarized zone. Everything to the north was Lebanon, and Syria was to the east.

A bee landed and worried over a blossom. The day bright, not a cloud in the sky, yet distant thunder boomed.

My sister-in-law walked down to me, her face registering concern. "Do you think those are guns?"

I doubt I fooled her when I changed the subject. We were safe where we were, but I'd wait till we were back in the van and far away before telling her she'd heard the Syrian civil war raging across the border and that Damascus was only about twenty-five miles away. Thirty-five hundred years ago clashing swords rang out here as Dan's boys attacked. Now the pop of gunfire and boom of barrel bombs ruled the day.

Yup, Solomon, same ol' sun. Wars and rumors of war. The tragedy of conflict and combat is bloody and heartbreaking, and I hate it with everything in me. . . .

We climbed a low hill behind the temple and skirted a eucalyptus grove by way of a rutted dirt road. Rusty barbed wire laced the brush. Down in an abandoned machine-gun bunker, we took a look around. Empty now, but well used in its day. A rusty old bunk still hung from the wall. In the days leading up to the Six-Day War in 1967, Israeli forces manned this place around the clock. Not a happy hangout back then. The big gun had to be manned every second of every day. I'd read about it, and standing there, I could picture it. Perfectly disciplined, without taking his eyes from the gun slit, a soldier would rouse his replacement from slumber by yanking a rope tied to the guy's leg. This cycle went on and on as long as the conflict lasted. Such was life in a concrete box, a few strands of barbed wire away from hell on earth.

Back in the sunlight, we skirted the back side of the grove and approached the ongoing excavation and preservation effort of Abraham's Gate. The site is one of Israel's most significant historical treasures, but it's out of the way enough to avoid most of the crowds. No ticketed entry. No roped-off lines. We were completely alone.

It floors me every time I see it—the very gate Abraham passed through on his mission to rescue his nephew, Lot. Talk about history! That was a long time ago. The Bronze Age, Canaanite Period. Only five hundred years, give or take, after Noah's flood. Jerusalem wasn't called Jerusalem then. It was simply Salem, ruled by a mysterious high priest named Melchizedek, a shadowy figure many suppose might have been a manifestation of Jesus Christ Himself.

They say a week in Israel is worth a yearlong study in a seminary.

And places like Abraham's Gate lead me to believe it. Standing there, listening to the day breathe, you get a real feel for the land, for the geography. Sunday school stories are no longer just stories. They are real events that happened in tangible places populated with living souls. I thought about Abraham and Sarah leaving their comfortable valley in Ur at the Lord's call and traveling west to unfamiliar Canaan, probably right through here. . . . About their hundred-plus years of tent dwelling, looking forward to that better—eternal—country. . . . About their dealings with Pharaoh and Abimelech because Sarah was so beautiful neither king could take his eyes off of her. . . . About their interaction with the angel of God and the promise of the blessing of nations to come from their offspring. . . .

South of where we stood at Abraham's Gate, in Hebron, is the Tomb of the Patriarchs—the land and the cave Abraham bought in which to bury the wife of his youth, even as he grieved over her body. The tomb is still there to this day, beneath the Ibrahimi Mosque. And farther south of that, out in the desert, the well Abraham dug when he sojourned in Beer Sheva.

Real people living real lives. People imperfect, just like you and me, but loved and remembered as the faithful of God.

Circling back, we jumped forward a thousand years and stopped at Dan's ancient entry, where King David is believed to have sat in judgment. In 1993 a stunning find was made here: an inscribed stone mentioning the house of David. Solid archaeological proof of the king's existence and further support for the veracity of Scripture.

Dan is a hard place to leave, but we still had a full day ahead and lots to see. We decided to take a shorter trail back toward the parking lot. We bumped into the machine-gunned Israelis again. We stopped and talked for a minute. One young girl, the same age as my daughter, told me they were on a tour of historical sites as part of their military training. They laughed and held up two-fingered peace signs as they took pictures of each other. Later, I knew, they'd be required to tour Yad Vashem, the World Holocaust Remembrance Center in Jerusalem. I'd seen similar groups of recruits do the same. The mood would be much different then.

Close by, a group of hijab-covered women waded in a shallow pool. They chatted in Arabic while their children splashed around them. They paid neither the soldiers nor us any mind.

Another round of bombs thundered in the east.

No one paused. No one flinched. No one even looked up.

I thought again about Abraham and Sarah and Lot. I thought about King David and Dan. Of Jeroboam and his seeker-friendly medicine show. I thought about Israeli soldiers cooling their cans of beer in the cold spring water during the Six-Day War. And Muslim women too modest to lift their dresses out of ankle-deep water.

I thought about beauty and death and children splashing beneath Solomon's rising and setting, rising and setting sun.

CHAPTER 12

A Little Angel
Offers Little Sins

Israel is beautiful. Rich in history, rich in spirit. Israel can move you to a spiritual high. Lift you to mountaintops. The Scriptures come to life. After all, Israel is God's place.

But be careful. Watch your step if you get off the bus and wander a bit. Even a little. You don't have to go far to have gone too far. Keep your eyes open—or maybe not—because there's a good chance you'll see things no one mentions in the brochures. Israel is still God's place, but step out into the night, and Israel just might break your heart.

Because, whether ultra-Orthodox, religious Zionist, traditional Jew, Palestinian, or secular, all Israelis are human. And humans are flawed, broken, fallen creatures. Israel is the world. Like every other place on the planet, from Thailand to Tacoma, the Holy Land has its own dark side. . . .

I was in the middle of a dream when someone shoved open the door to my third-floor room of the little Tel Aviv travel hostel. Heart pounding, I covered my eyes against the hallway's bright florescent blaze. A thin guy stood in the doorway, tattooed and shirtless. He took in the room, then me, with a look of confusion.

"Ah, man, wrong room. Sorry," he said in a dead-ringer Captain Jack Sparrow accent.

"Yeah. No problem," I mumbled.

He closed the door behind him.

For a while I tried to go back to sleep. Not happening. Wide awake, I rolled out of my bottom bunk and fumbled around for some shorts and a t-shirt. I slid into my flip-flops and wandered down the hall to the communal bathroom. Steam rose from a few occupied shower stalls. Captain Jack stumbled in while I brushed my teeth. I nodded at him. He picked up a paper cup from the counter, filled it with cold water from the tap, then dumped it over the top of one of the shower curtains. What resulted was a loud string of four-letter words from the occupant, a litany as colorful as it was long—the guy had skills.

I rinsed and spit. "Friend of yours?"

"Yeah, he's a mate. Crazy night, man." His eyes were glazed. He tossed a few choice words of his own at the closed curtain. He laughed, then put his finger to his lips, inviting me in on his brilliant conspiracy, and filled the cup again.

I left the pirates to their profanity-riddled fun and headed for the front door of the hostel. At the bottom of the entry stairs, I spun the wheel to port and sailed south. Across the street a wide beach held back the Mediterranean. I could hear the waves, but it was still too dark to see the water.

Tel Aviv isn't the Israel most Westerners imagine. It's not the black-hatted Orthodox bobbing prayers at the Wailing Wall. Or the peaceful beauty of Gethsemane. Tel Aviv is Israel's version of New York or San Francisco. One part luxury, two parts grunge, Tel Aviv is a fast-moving, metropolitan insomniac. A jittery junkie looking for the next fix.

I paused at the corner beneath a night sky fading into the deep-blue divination of dawn. A man swept the sidewalk. Music thumped from a hole-in-the-wall falafel place behind him. Whether starting or ending his day, I couldn't tell. Colorful business cards littered the ground in all directions. They're called tart cards, a familiar sight in Middle Eastern carpe diem playgrounds like Tel Aviv and Eilat. I'd seen them before. They're hard to miss. Women, scantily clad, in every imaginable sexually acrobatic pose. The cards would be there awhile longer, but by the time the latest wave of cargo-pantsed, sun-hatted tourists had their breakfasts and hit the street to load onto buses headed for Jerusalem, Tiberias, or the Dead Sea, most of the cards would have vanished. After all, this is the Holy Land, and appearances are important.

While various laws work to keep a lid on the very real problem of human trafficking and abuse of underage girls, the act of prostitution itself has been legal in Israel since 1949. Littering is another story. You can get fined for that—though I don't think anyone mentioned it to the army of bike messengers, each paid a hundred shekels or so to drop a thousand cards on the streets every night.

Business is hopping and competition is fierce. The ugly fact is, hundreds of brothels operate openly in Tel Aviv alone, even though organized prostitution is illegal. Many call it an "open secret," but it's a massive black eye as far as religious tourism is concerned. According to a 2016 article in the Israeli newspaper *Haaretz*, a government study discovered there are up to 12,730 sex workers in Israel, with each having an estimated 660 clients a year. That means people (mostly men) on average make 700,150 visits to prostitutes each month. An amazing and horrible number—and one that I suspect is well below the actual stats.

Seedy? Yes. Sad? Horribly. Profitable? Definitely. The sex industry in the Holy Land reels in over *$500 million* a year.

I read an article once in which the writer recalled picking a card up from a Tel Aviv street. The Hebrew lettering said, "A Little Angel Offers Little Sins." That spoke volumes to me. Despite the laws and the well-meaning efforts of rescue organizations and street ministries, many of the girls working the sex trade are just that—little girls. A little angel offers little sins: alcohol, drugs, abuse, rape—all in an angelic day's (or night's) work.

I've seen the women on the Tel Aviv streets on late-night runs to the airport. Every shape, size, and hair color. They sleep in doorways and alleys. They wander, eyes haunted and hollow. Rudyard Kipling called prostitution the world's oldest profession. I imagine that's true. The devil has been around since the beginning, preying on the weak and wounded. Preying on *the least of these*.

Drugs, sex, violence—Satan uses all the colors on his palette. And exhibits of his artwork aren't hard to find in Tel Aviv. Across the street I saw the Dolphinarium discotheque, abandoned since 2001 when a Hamas suicide bomb turned it into a burned-out shell. A good example. The woman in a shelter bed beneath the bus station, her leg half eaten away with infection from a dirty heroin needle, another. Sometimes the enemy of our souls is subtle, loving us to him, thrilling our spirits with soft, beautiful heresy. Sometimes he comes with thundering rage and carrying a nail-studded club.

Satan does whatever it takes.

I turned to make my way back toward the hotel. I thought I might go back to bed, catch another hour of sleep, but I changed my mind. I wasn't tired. With dawn officially broken, I opted for a cup of coffee instead. I watched the ocean turn from black to purple to blue. I thought of my own precious daughter safely back home in Idaho.

Jaffa, the oldest seaport in the world, was only a twenty-minute walk south from my coffee cup. Jesus's disciple Peter had a vision there two thousand years ago: he saw the gospel of Truth and Grace as being available to the whole world, Jew and Gentile alike. He must have passed very closely to where I sat on his way to share that vision with Cornelius just up the road in Caesarea Maritima. Was Peter's day any different? Brighter? More innocent? I don't imagine so. Where man is, sin will abound.

But—just as Peter found out when he saw that sheet come down—where sin abounds, grace abounds even more.

I don't think Peter would be shocked over tart cards. Grieved, maybe, but not surprised. He'd tell us to remember, no matter what slogan is painted on the side of the bus, we're not tourists in this world but pilgrims, mere travelers. And life doesn't offer a ride of air-conditioned comfort, stopping along the way only for the good stuff. No, we have to get off and walk once in a while. Sometimes out there it gets dark, and we lose the path for a minute or two. When we do, there's a good chance of bumping into mean, ugly things. Things we never expected when we were in our own, personal Holy Land world. We step around a corner, and suddenly life punches us in the face. Hopefully we climb up out of the dust stronger than before.

Sometimes we're stubborn. Sometimes we walk with our hands out in front of us, blinded by scales of sin. After all, we are human.

We are weak. But God will be God: He can't change. His eye is on the sparrow . . . and on the lowest sinner. On mountaintops and in valleys, through the miles, He is there, offering love before we ask. He rejoices in our joy. He weeps in our pain because He knows what it is to suffer. When we can't take another step, He smiles, and should we choose, He will pick us up and carry us in His arms.

And He is there, where a red light burns on a narrow, dark Tel Aviv street, His heart broken to pieces for a little angel.

Please pray for her.

CHAPTER 13

Just Lean Back

There's a water tower down in the bottom corner of California next to Mexico that says Welcome to El Centro. I remember it being there back when I was a kid, down the highway from where I grew up. It had a "Sea Level" line painted on it about halfway up. That kind of freaked me out. What if the West Coast sprang a leak or something? Everyone would drown, right?

El Centro sits about forty feet below sea level. Death Valley, California, two hundred feet below. The Dead Sea on the Israeli-Jordanian border, *thirteen hundred* feet below sea level.

That's low.

The first time I saw the Dead Sea area, I felt like I was back in the bleak and barren Mojave Desert around Yuma, Arizona, where I grew up and out. I could have been driving down through California's Imperial Valley next to the Salton Sea. Date palms, scattered fields, drip irrigation—the same desert with its sharp, rocky peaks in the distance. The Salton Sea is saline and mineral rich. A few hardy fish live there. The Dead Sea is the Salton Sea on steroids. No fish live there. Not even a guppy.

And yet the place teems with life. You have to love Israel.

Our first trip to the Dead Sea was a rainy and cold undertaking. Unnaturally so, they told us. We'd shivered our way through Jerusalem and Galilee. We hoped for a little sun and warmth in the south.

Not happening.

But . . . Michelle and I were in Israel. And who knew? We might never have a chance to come back.

So we stood on the empty beach and looked out at the Dead Sea.

"What do you think?" I said.

"I think it's cold," she answered.

"Yeah, let's bag it."

"No way! We're here. We gotta do it."

Bill Perkins, our tour leader, came up. "You guys going out there? You gonna float?"

"Debating," I said.

"We're definitely going out there," Michelle said.

"You got your suits?" Bill said.

I had to admit we did. Then I had a brainstorm. "But we don't have towels. Oh well, too bad." I knew Michelle likes a nice towel.

Bill walked off and came back a couple minutes later with two brand-new towels. "Here."

"You bought these?" I said.

"Your wife wants to float in the Dead Sea," he said, "so you gotta float in the Dead Sea."

"Then I guess I'll float in the Dead Sea," I said.

"Cool. I'll watch. It's cold," Bill said.

Bill's a stand-up guy.

Michelle and I went into some changing rooms.

"A lot of people will probably do it, right?" she said. "We're only here once."

"Yeah, I'm sure a bunch of them will."

A bunch of them didn't.

Thirty people stood on the beach, arms crossed against the cold, while Michelle and I—alone—took the long walk to the water.

No last-minute call from the governor. No stay of execution. Just a slow death. . . . Death by cold, oily salt water.

Toes . . . ankles . . . knees . . .

"Just lean back and sit down!" Bill called, demonstrating his stand-up-guy side again.

"They're all watching us," Michelle said under her breath.

"Let's get it over with," I said.

We did.

We floated.

We looked at each other.

"Weird," I said.

"Definitely weird," Michelle said.

"Cold?" I said.

"Definitely cold. Freezing."

"Done?"

"Definitely done."

Hey, if you're only there once. . . .

But we've been several times since. Several *warm* times.

On our last trip we had a few friends and family who wanted to do the Dead Sea bob. No problem. A sleepy security guy opened the community gate for us, and we rolled down toward the water. Welcome to Ein Bokek. A hedonistic strip of desert life wedged between the deceptively refreshing-looking turquoise water of the Dead

Sea and the red-brown bluffs of the Judean Desert. Expensive shopping, several luxury hotels, even a McDonald's. Moses and the kids did forty years' worth of wandering south of here. Just to the north Aaron took them into the promised land. These days, I guess Quarter Pounders and shakes trump manna and quail.

Shopping is expensive, but the beach is free. Like any good beach should be. I fished for shekels for the parking meter—that part's not free—while the group headed for the sand. I caught snatches of Hebrew, Arabic, and a lot of Russian on the hot breeze. Ein Bokek is a big Russian tourist destination. A tour bus rolled to a stop, air-brakes sighing. Fifty or so people filed out. They looked American, but Australian accents said otherwise. Another bus parked. Chinese this time.

Every day at Ein Bokek is Multicultural Day.

The Chinese group milled around the bus applying copious amounts of sunscreen to each other and accepting beach towels the tour guide passed out from the cargo hold. I followed the Australians down to the beach. The place was crowded.

I remember once, back in Arizona as a kid, my dad talking weather with a farmer friend of his. That day it was 120 degrees in the shade. "Yeah," the old guy said, eyes squinting beneath the brim of his cowboy hat, "but it's only 115 with the wind chill."

That pretty much summed it up for Ein Bokek. The beach was dry and October-in-Israel-desert hot. Baking. A far cry from our first polar bear plunge. I found my group in the shade of a cabana stripping down to their suits. We stuffed clothes into bags and backpacks and tossed them up onto the low roof for safekeeping.

I paused at the edge of the water and looked out. On a busy day the Dead Sea can be weird. A watery Twilight Zone field sprouting a crop of round faces under broad-brimmed sun hats. There must have been a hundred of them out there, bobbing in sync and looking back toward the beach.

The air rumbled. Then the ground shook. From the south came three jet fighters screaming low over the water in perfect formation. A hundred sunburned mushrooms rotated a 180 degrees to watch.

Michelle went in with Yvette, her sister, so I shuffled out on my own. The sea looked cool, beautiful, inviting. Caribbean crystal turquoise.

A beautiful illusion.

The actual water was up over ninety degrees. Still, it felt cool compared to the air. Salt crunched beneath my flip-flops. The oily water made the rubber slick, so I took them off and carried them. I didn't need Bill to tell me, "Just lean back." I had it down this time.

The feeling of being in the Dead Sea never fails to surprise. *Weird*. I settled into the warm, watery armchair and used my flip-flops to paddle out backward. After a while I stopped and bobbed. Then bobbed some more. A minute or two later, the initial *weird* fading, I found myself completely bored. A few yards away a book-reading mushroom bobbed. I thought she might be one of the Australians.

"What are you reading?" I said. "Any good?"

Her eyes flicked my direction then back to the book.

Oh well. I felt around on the seabed with my toes for salt balls. Certain times of the year, there are quite a few. Anywhere from the size of a marble to the size of a tennis ball. I like to take a couple home. Nothing that day, though. (I *did* find a long, salt-encrusted clump of hair. *Better than nothing* didn't apply.)

The jets screamed by again. I turned to watch with the rest of the mushrooms.

"Seems like they're doing a loop. Come by about every ten minutes," I said to the bobbing bookworm.

No response.

I gave it one more try. "Water's weird, isn't it?"

She dropped a hand paddle into the water and put ten extra feet between us.

G'day, mate, I said to myself.

I bobbed some more.

The hotels rose into the sky, gleaming as they reflected the desert sun. It's an odd place to describe, really. Families vacation there alongside the partiers. Teenagers hang out in the mall shops, McDonald's, and coffeehouses. All very Western. Prostitutes often solicit in the middle of the day. It's a big, hot, swirling mill of innocence and sin, located within a stone's throw of the scorched remains of biblical Sodom and Gomorrah. The landscape probably looked a lot different in Abraham and Lot's day, but we humans haven't changed a whole lot.

I looked out at the water. The *Dead* Sea. A liquid ghost town. Even the piles of driftwood along the shore looked like bleached bones. On every level, sin and hopelessness blanketed the place.

And I smiled.

Because I know Him.

Because it's always in the deadest places—be it the moonscape of the Negev, the hard-packed earth of a hippodrome floor, or the salty depths of a broken soul—that the God of love insists on breathing new life.

See, Ezekiel prophesied a glorious day. A day when fresh, pure water would flow from Jerusalem in the east and rush this death with life. When the Dead Sea's waters would teem with fish and other living things. A beautiful oasis once again. A day when something hopeless becomes the glory of what it was meant to be.

I've seen the same miracle burst to light and life in a thousand dead souls. Including mine.

Back on shore I stood underneath the freshwater shower for a long time. A lot cooler than the seawater. I toweled off in the shade of the cabana where my mom and mother-in-law stood watching the rest of the group, still out in the water. We were in no hurry.

My nephew slogged in.

"Whaddya think, Dwaner?" His name is Dane, which translates to *Dwaner* in unclespeak.

"It's really weird," he said.

"That's what I think. You talk to any Australians?"

"No."

"Neither did I."

A couple overweight guys shuffled by in speedos.

"That's weird, too," Dane said.

"Yup."

My sister Deni, a world-class professional photographer, snapped a few covert shots for her *Speedos of the World* collection. A wonderful and deep piece of art, if you ask me.

The Chinese group filed by on their way back to the bus, all smiles and excited chattering. I don't know how to say *weird* in Chinese, but if I did, I'll bet you a million shekels I would have heard it more than once.

Low thunder rumbled.

The jets roared by again.

I looked around one last time, enjoying the ever-presence of Jesus. I knew that thirty or so miles to the north and east in Jerusalem, just beyond the thick walls of the Old City—and the paper-thin wall of human space, time, and consciousness—a torrent of Living Water roiled and swelled, just waiting for its time to flood this place with life.

What will they call the Dead Sea then?

CHAPTER 14

Bacon Cheeseburgers and the Man of the Hour

My friend Chik fancies himself a *foodie*. He's right. I've tagged along to a few restaurants with him, and when it comes to culinary excellence, you can take Chik's word to the bank.

Chik swears you can get the best bacon cheeseburger in the world in Jerusalem. I think that's crazy, but Chik would know. He can also give you directions to the best tattoo parlor in Israel. Chik's like that. A fountain of information.

Everyone who knows Chik will tell you he's also a walking adventure.

Chik is not shy. He probably got a Hebrew tattoo while eating a bacon cheeseburger.

In a crowded room . . . or auditorium . . . or stadium, you can always find him. You just have to listen. Or look for the big crowd of kids.

No, Chik is not quiet. Chik is fun.

One night my cell phone rang as I walked with some friends from the Jewish to the Armenian Quarter in the Old City. An Israeli phone number flashed on the screen. I answered. Chik's voice, sounding like he was next door.

He didn't say hello. Just "Buck, you're in Jerusalem, right? Where are you right now?"

"Um, walking back from the Jewish Quarter on our way to Christ Church, where we're staying. Are you here?"

"Yeah. We're having a worship night with you tonight. Hurry up. We're at the Imperial Hotel."

"Tonight as in *tonight*?"

"I didn't stutter, brother."

I wasn't positive as to exactly where the Imperial Hotel was, though I knew it was close by. "Man, Chik, I hiked Masada early this morning, and we've been walking the Old City all day since. I'm wiped out. Can we do it tomorrow?"

"Nope, we're all waiting for you. It'll be great."

"I'm not even sure where the Imperial is."

"Yup. It's gonna be great."

"I'm talking *dead on my feet* tired. As in *not a little*."

"Perfect. Gonna be great. . . . Imperial."

"Man, I don't think we're even having the same conversation."

"Exactly. See you in a few." Such is Chik.

"I'm not sure where the Imperial is. How do I find you?"

"You're on your way into the Armenian Quarter?"

"Uh-huh."

"Finding me won't be a problem."

I wasn't sure what he meant by that. Not sure I wanted to know. But, true to his claim, it wasn't a problem. We were somewhere on Armenian Patriarchate Street when my mother-in-law said, "Did you just hear someone call your name?"

"I don't think so."

But then I *did* hear it. Someone shouting my name. . . . Then shouting it again—over and over . . . and over. . . . As we walked on, the voice got louder. "Buck Storm!" was echoing and booming down the stone walls and streets of the Old City.

Chik said I'd be able to find him. That was one way to do it.

Like I said, Chik is not quiet.

After a while we spotted him standing in the middle of the street in front of the Tower of David, handlebar mustache at attention, shouting my name at the top of his lungs. A small crowd of curious onlookers had gathered.

Chik grinned when he saw me. "I told you you'd find me. You ready?"

I had to laugh.

My legs reminded me again about my 5:00 a.m. Masada hike. My body begged for a hot shower and a bed. And, at that very moment, both of those were less than a hundred feet from where I stood. "Wait! You know what? I don't have a guitar here."

"Yup, got ya covered. You ready? Let's go."

Adios, bed. Guess I was going to the Imperial. You don't fight Hurricane Chik. Many a brave mariner has gone down doing just that. Best to reef your mainsail and ride the wind.

"Let me go get my people settled," I told him.

"No prob. Hurry." He gave me quick, loose directions to the Imperial and then Chik-ed off into the nighttime streets of Jerusalem.

Most of my group, seriously tired, headed for their rooms, but a brave few opted to tag along. With the others settled, we started out.

Chik had given loose directions, and by "loose" I mean we wound up at the *Gloria* instead of the *Imperial*. But I was so tired by that point I couldn't remember what hotel he'd said. *Maybe the Gloria? Maybe not? Sounded sort of right.* Anyway, I'd heard about the Gloria, and I was glad to check it out. A cool, old-world place. All stone and archways and uncertain, yellow light. In fact, we got to check all of it out, every single floor, looking for Chik and company, my rubber Masada legs cursing me on every stair. We even walked into a couple wrong gatherings. Neither of them appeared enthusiastic about party crashers. Finally, we emerged onto the roof. If you ever have the chance, get lost in Jerusalem and check out the skyline from the Gloria Hotel roof. Tell you what. If you're disappointed, I'll buy you a bacon cheeseburger.

The Gloria dumped us out onto the street Chik-less and confused. I broke down and called him.

"Where are you?" he said.

"At the Gloria, like you said."

"I said the Imperial."

Oh yeah, the Imperial. . . .

"Right. Where's the Imperial again?"

Turns out we'd walked right past the Imperial. Twice. We passed through the lobby and up a flight of a jillion stairs. The room wasn't huge, but, sure enough, Chik had a good group gathered. Lots of young people burned from the day and the sun but excited about Jesus and Jerusalem. I knew several of them from a worship workshop I'd done in Omaha a couple months or so prior. Others I knew from visiting Chik's church out in St. Paul a few times. Beautiful people, sincere hearts. Worshippers.

A stool waited. Somebody handed me a guitar. I played a song or two I'd written about Israel. They listened politely, but I saw something different in their eyes. As I realized the night refused a

Buck Storm concert, Jerusalem kicked me back to *me* like an out-of-bounds soccer ball. Something bigger was pressing. Insisting. So I started to worship. An old Roby Duke song felt right.

He shall reign
Forever and ever
The Lord omnipotent praise His name
Forever amen

That clicked. Chik's sunburned choir opened up and sang along with the angels. Turns out, Jesus was the Man of the hour. As it should be.

After a while I passed the guitar over, and someone else took it and started a song. The instrument continued around the room, and voices echoed through the halls of the Imperial . . . and of heaven itself.

This worship warmed my soul. I think it warmed theirs too. There we were, in Old Jerusalem, in an upper room, just a looping line drive away from Calvary, waiting on, and in communion with, the King of kings. We lingered long. I wasn't tired anymore.

At length I said goodnight to my friends. We all had an early morning coming. My group, slated to explore more of Jerusalem, and Chik's off to a struggling Christian church somewhere deep in the West Bank.

It was late. Back out on the street, things were quiet. A light breeze tugged, clean and cool. The heat of the day just a memory. We walked down the street and buzzed at Christ Church's iron gates. They opened. My friends headed for their rooms. I skirted the building toward mine, the garden air filled with grace and the scent of growing things. I climbed the stairs and tried my best to be quiet when I went in so I wouldn't wake Michelle.

I showered and lay down next to my wife, mind still full of the evening. Soft light filtered through the window high up in the wall. I heard what sounded like distant gunfire. A helicopter thumped by overhead. A dog barked.

Jerusalem. . . .

I knew I'd never forget that night.

Imperial—*royal, kingly.* Gloria—*glory.* Specifically *God's* glory. Even the names of the hotels point to the One who will one day— maybe soon—take His throne in that city. A day when every knee will bow and every tongue confess that Jesus Christ is the Son of God, that He alone is Lord. I wish it could be today. But His timing isn't my timing. He's patient, He's kind, desiring and drawing all men without respect to wall, border, language, culture, religion. . . . He knows we were all created to sing His name.

Yes, one day *every* tongue. . . .

But as for me? I won't wait, brother. I'm on my knees.

He shall reign.

CHAPTER 15

Bombs

My wife isn't a chain coffee shop person. Unless we're in a pinch, Starbucks is out, Jack. And there's a three-inch stack of local-coffee-joint punch cards in the center console of our car to testify. It doesn't matter where we are in the country—in a city or a small town—she's got a punch card. Clarinda, Iowa; Payson, Arizona; Seattle—she pulls out her stack and thumbs through, saying, "Wait! I have a card for here somewhere." The crazy thing is, she usually does.

I don't mind Starbucks if we're in a hurry. At least the quality is consistent. I'll admit, however, there are exceptions. For instance, if you find yourself on the dock waiting for a ship in Kuşadası, Turkey, ignore the mermaid on that green and white sign. Trust me, that siren's song will drag you straight onto the rocks of disgusting. I'm not sure what it was they gave me there, but one sip and that sucker went straight over the rail to Davy Jones's locker. I'm surprised Davy didn't spit it back.

Truck-stop coffee will get you through a long night across the South Dakota badlands. Or up the California I-5 corridor with the ghosts of Buck Owens and Steinbeck whipping alongside. Even church coffee is getting better all the time thanks to every fellowship in American suburbia starting "Coffee Ministries"—either *He Brews* or *Holy Grounds,* depending on the denominational bent.

I've never been to a Starbucks in Central America, but I love the coffee there. Here's a little traveler's tip. Duck into any café or market and say the words *café negro, por favor.* Angels will start singing.

All that to say, drop a pin on a world map, Michelle and I will manage to find a place for coffee. In Israel we usually look for the big black cup stuck on a pole. (I like it when they make it easy.) Beneath that big black cup you'll find a Café Aroma. Kind of like the pot of gold at the end of the rainbow except it actually exists. Like I said, we're not chain people, but even my wife makes an exception for Café Aroma. Kind of Israel's answer to Starbucks—if Starbucks served excellent Italian private roast.

Starbucks, in fact, opened six locations in Israel in 2001. They closed all six in 2003. I've heard people offer a few different reasons for this. Who knows, maybe Israelis don't like pumpkin spice lattes. (Then again, does anybody?) When someone I'm traveling with in Israel asks to stop at one of the McDonald's dotting the country, I find some mom-and-pop falafel or shawarma place. When they ask if there's a Starbucks, I find the big black cup. You ask, "Why did Starbucks fold after two years?" I say, "How did they last that long?"

Italian roast, Turkish coffee, bitter Greek brew—the coffee culture in Israel is as different as it is superior. In Israel coffee drinking is social. Israelis aren't so much paper cup on-the-go types. They tend to sit. Plant themselves over actual ceramic mugs and spend time talking to one another. I love that.

And it's exactly what I found myself doing on a cool, spring day in Jerusalem. I was sitting across a patio table from an Israeli bus driver at the Mount Scopus Café Aroma. Michelle was inside chatting with a tour guide, so he and I were alone. He had a mug; I had a paper cup. His, an espresso; mine, an Americano. (I still can't decide whether that was poetic or cliché.) I commented on the amount of security around the place. We'd had to come through metal detectors on the way in.

He pointed to the Hebrew University across the street. "You never know, eh?"

True, you never know.

And in that part of the world, you never take another breath for granted.

On July 31, 2002, Hamas terrorists detonated a bomb in the Hebrew University cafeteria, killing nine people (five of them were American) and wounding another hundred.

My bus driver friend seemed lost in thought or memories or both. I asked him what it was like living with the constant threat of terror. I couldn't imagine.

He studied me for a long second or two. "These are evil people. There is no one in Israel who has not been touched by terrorism. Everyone knows someone, or knows someone who knows someone, who has been killed or injured."

He looked down at his cup. I had the feeling he wanted to say more. I sipped my Americano and waited. Some issues are too personal to press. This was definitely one. And, after all, who was I to ask?

At length he said, "You heard about the Café Moment bombing?"

"I don't think so." I felt bad saying so.

Lines creased his forehead. He didn't speak for a long time, and I began to suspect the line of conversation might be over. Something in his face shifted. His eyes narrowed a fraction as he gazed out across the street. I had the feeling he summoned something down deep. In a moment he transformed from bus driver to tough ex-IDF. The metamorphosis happened right in front of me. A physical act of the man's will.

"A very horrible thing. My best friend and his girlfriend were there. They were killed that night," he said.

"I'm sorry," I said. "I can't imagine." And I couldn't.

"Only a couple days later, as soon as they cleared the bodies and wreckage away, they set up plywood tables and began serving again. They did this to show that we are a strong people. We won't be bullied. The terrorists are cowards. Let me ask you, where is the honor in killing innocents? My friends? They never hurt anyone. These people blow up cafés, but that's not enough, so they blow up our buses and our trains." He pointed across the street. "They blow up our universities. They aren't killing armed combatants. They target children and housewives. What kind of *people* do that? What kind of *evil* does that?"

I felt small. Horribly humbled. This wasn't walking through a historical site listening to a guide and taking cell phone pictures. It wasn't some disconnected third-page headline from the other side of the world. This was right here, right now. Human loss and pain on a grand scale. And this quiet man chose to share it with me. The world shrank. Sitting across the table from him, sharing coffee, I felt his problems were my problems now. His pain, my pain. I was right there in it. Part of it.

"What . . . in your opinion . . . can be done?" I said, struggling to keep my voice sounding neutral.

He shrugged. "We build a wall to protect ourselves, but the world demands we take it down. Saying we are oppressing the Palestinians.

Occupying. How can we be *occupying* our own country? What did the world say after Café Moment? As we were cleaning blood and body parts off the walls? Nothing. Not a word. So we live. What else can we do? We rebuild. We take our children to the park. We fight when we can . . . if we have to. We are talking about our home here. We go on with our lives because we can't let them win." His face softened again, soldier was now driver. "Look, you had the World Trade Center attack. It is no longer only an Israeli problem. It is a world problem. You will see." He picked up his espresso and changed the subject.

Later, I looked up the Café Moment bombing. March 9, 2002. A Saturday night. Only a hundred meters from Prime Minister Benjamin Netanyahu's home. The Hamas-sponsored suicide bomber walked into the crowded café and detonated his vest. Eleven killed, fifty-four wounded. Evil done in the name of God. Some of the Muslim world partied. The rest of the world stayed mostly silent. Or, par for the course, actually blamed the Israelis.

Well over three million tourists visit Israel every year, and they are almost never directly affected by the religious/political conflict. Tourism is big business, and business means income no matter which side of the religious/political fence you're standing on. Most visitors will tell you they've never felt more secure than when they were in Israel. I'm glad. They *should* feel safe. After all, God knows our days. But should you ever find yourself in Israel, take some time and talk with the people. Ask them what they hope for, what they want for their future, for their children's future. Ask them about their fears. Take some time to show them that not all of the three million people tromping through their country are only there to shop, take pictures, and *take* in general.

Give instead.

Give your heart; give your time. Let them know they are not alone. Give them Jesus.

Michelle and I took a taxi to Ben Yehuda Street, a popular and hopping pedestrian area in the heart of downtown Jerusalem. It was Saturday night, the end of Shabbat, a time to celebrate. A time to relax and enjoy life.

I had a hard time putting the coffeehouse conversation out of my head. Busy places make good terrorist targets, and Ben Yehuda Street has seen its share. As we walked, I watched the people. Street musicians played. People danced. A line of restaurant patrons laughed and chatted as they waited to pass through a metal detector on the way to dinner. A choir of American teenagers sang worship songs.

Life went on. What else can life do?

I thought about the bus driver's story and how strange it all was. Two children are born. Both have a family who loves them. They grow. They play with their friends. They both put posters of their sports heroes on the walls of their rooms. They both have a crush on a pretty girl. Who knows? Maybe the same girl.

And one day they both find themselves in a café.

One is drinking coffee.

One mumbles a prayer.

One laughs at a joke.

One pushes a button.

Both are gone.

In a Jerusalem apartment, a mother and father wail their grief. In a West Bank apartment, a different set of parents proudly hang wreaths of flowers on a portrait.

This is not God.

And this is not human.

Michelle and I stepped into a shop. Quieter there than out on the street. We looked around for a while. I noticed a plaque on the wall behind the sales counter and moved toward it to get a better look. Twisted nails, bolts, and bits of jagged metal were mounted around an inscription. Shrapnel, it explained, from a car bomb detonated just outside the front door in 2001. Thank You for Coming and Supporting Israel, the plaque said at the bottom. The fact it was written in English left no doubt whom it was written to.

The young cashier handed us our change and smiled. "Thank you," she said.

"You're very welcome."

CHAPTER 16

Found in Translation

During a concert back sometime in the early 2000s, I finished my set, put my guitar on a stand, and walked off the stage. It was a warm day in Phoenix, but in the auditorium, the air conditioner hummed, keeping the room almost chilly. I took a seat in the back and watched the next speaker step up to the podium. A pastor named Bradley, from Jerusalem, a place I'd always wanted to see. Bradley greeted people and then talked a bit about Calvary Chapel Jerusalem and For Zion's Sake, the ministry he oversaw. As I listened, I thought he seemed distracted, the whole thing was a little disjointed. I couldn't quite put my finger on it, but something was definitely there.

I'd never met Bradley, but I liked him right off. I found myself rooting for him like you root for a comedian who hasn't quite pulled in the audience yet. He talked awhile, explaining his church's humanitarian work in Jerusalem, an outreach to the *Olim*, those Jews from around the globe who are making *Aliyah*, who are moving to Israel, often arriving with nothing more than the clothes on their backs.

The talk about Israel—the history, the geography, the people, how it all integrated with Scripture—held my interest for a while.

But, honestly, it had been a late travel night and an early morning. I found myself mentally drifting. . . .

Christian conferences can be interesting and impactful . . . or not. Sometimes, I'm afraid, intellectualism, high theology, and political soapboxing push aside the broken heart of Jesus for His beloved. But the beautiful thing about Jesus is that He has no book table in the lobby. No CDs or DVDs to sell. He doesn't need them. He shares His stage with no man. He *will* press in.

And He did that day.

Because Bradley—far from soapboxing—was humble and obedient.

I remember something in his voice shifting. He paused, leaned forward, hands on the podium, and bowed his head for a long moment. He took a long look around the room. Then he opened a Bible and began to read.

I don't remember him giving any explanation for the sudden jerk of the steering wheel. He might have. I *do* remember being immediately pulled from my air-conditioned drowse.

Bradley read a psalm of David. Simply. No commentary offered. The broken king's deep, sincere groaning of repentance and supplication, penned thousands of years ago, reached through the millennia and spoke intimately and directly, pulling us out of sleepy pride. Out of ourselves. Into Him.

Bradley's voice caught with emotion. This psalm *meant* something to him. He read on.

And as he read, a miracle. David's heart became God's heart. And Bradley's heart became God's heart. I heard a woman near me begin to cry softly. Then another. The psalm, the gathering, God's immediate presence—all intertwined. I found myself undone.

After the psalm, Bradley went on to teach again for a while, I think. The history of the Jews. God's plan for Israel in these last days. I'm sure it was good. But I'd already been taught. Wrapped up and spinning in a swirl of ancient supplication, I'd been held in the arms of God, my face on His shoulder, His breath on my cheek.

Later that afternoon I found myself standing next to Bradley in the crowd. He shook my hand and said how much he'd enjoyed the music. I wanted to tell him about my experience. I tried, but I don't think I came across the way I'd hoped. Sometimes those tender, skin-to-skin moments with our Maker are so personal they can't be explained. Still, Bradley and I definitely connected that day over the heart of Christ.

"If you're ever in Jerusalem, come play at the church." He said it like Jerusalem might be the next town down the highway.

"I'll be there," I told him. I meant it.

A couple years later, Jerusalem was exactly where I found myself, guitar in hand. My very first experience traveling the Holy Land. I'd emailed Bradley before we left. He was in Switzerland but said I should come anyway. He'd arrange with the staff my visit to his church.

So I went.

After a long day of touring amazing places, several of us loaded back onto the bus and drove to Bradley's church. I wasn't sure what to expect. I'd been to a thousand churches in America but never to a single one in Israel. It was different from what I'd pictured, this out-of-the-way industrial-looking place.

The man covering for Bradley was nice but clearly confused. It was evident right away something had been lost in translation. An email somewhere had bounced off a wrong satellite. Maybe a little church in Thailand or Wales or Nashville might be expecting me, but in Bradley's church on that rainy night in Jerusalem, I was a total surprise.

The man apologized profusely.

"No problem!" I said, and I meant it. I certainly didn't have to play that night. We'd be happy just to join the service.

"No, no," he said. "Please, come in. Please play us something. Encourage us."

I was surprised to see that, when we walked into the sanctuary, our little bus group more than doubled the congregation. They introduced me in English, and I walked up onto the little stage. I felt out of place. Awkward. A little embarrassed. All I really wanted to do was sit down. In my heart I silently let God know exactly that.

I knew His voice when it came: *Are you confused? Are you under the impression this is somehow about you? You are here. Now do what I have for you to do.* I also knew the familiar and disconcerting feeling of being part of something outside myself. Something bigger. Something infinitely better.

So I told Him I was sorry.

And I played.

I started with a song about my grandfather called "The Fisherman's Song." A story of God showing love through the obedience of a simple man. I talked a little, shared what came to mind. I paused at intervals as a few different people translated to small clusters of gatherers. Hebrew, Spanish, and Russian. . . . Then I played another song. Down to my right a handful of hard-looking young men in front of the Russian interpreter leaned forward, forearms on their knees, listening with serious intensity. I looked down into their faces. An eagerness there. Hunger. I felt the Father's love for them. As I played, I knew none of them understood the words, but something happened in that room that night. Something spiritual. Something wonderful.

Everyone felt it.

Maybe music actually is the language of the angels. Sometimes I suspect it is, but I don't know. I do know music transcends human description. It moves back and forth with unapologetic impunity between the physical and spiritual. They say it's the universal language. Some people present in Jerusalem that night said it was. They credited the gift of music with transcending borders and backgrounds and communication barriers.

But, between you and me, I don't think it was music that night at all.

Something deeper than rhythm, chords, and melody happened to us there. Deep called out to deep in that place. Father called to His children. He held us. He whispered His love. He promised eternity.

It all seemed surreal to me. To this day I remember it like a dream. As if I watched the whole thing from a distance. This is not a story of me. I was inconsequential at best. Nothing but ethereal mist. A spirit haunting my tiny, allotted earthly space while the God of the universe—the only genuinely real and eternal Being—ministered peace and comfort to the saints in Jerusalem.

We talked for a long time after, unified in the presence of Christ. In the rich and life-giving fellowship of believers. I believe in my heart God rejoiced in our midst. Maybe, if we'd listened closely, we could have heard His song of joy echoing through the Jerusalem sky.

At a recent event I played, a woman who'd happened to be in that room that night approached me as I put my guitar in its case. I hadn't seen her in years. I stood and we hugged.

"Do you remember when I got lost in the Old City, left at that restaurant, and you came back to find me?"

I told her I did.

She smiled and said, "Do you remember that night when you played at that little church in Jerusalem?" she said.

I told her I did. And that I'd never forget it.

She put a hand on my arm. "You know, out of all the amazing things we saw, all the places we went, that night was the most special to me. It was the thing I remember most—the feeling of God's presence. I still think about it all the time."

She wasn't the first, second, or even third person to tell me the same. And I knew it wasn't *me* she complimented, which made her statement the greatest compliment of all.

Why? I can't speak for everyone there that night, but I suspect, for each of us in our own way, the story is the same. It goes like this:

One cool, wet night in Jerusalem, a group of pilgrims got off their tour bus to visit an important site. One well off the usual tour route. A place rarely visited by outsiders. A site more solid and sturdy than Herod's temple stones. More ancient than Abraham's Gate, Babylon, or even Eden. No tour guide's flag led them there. No gift shop beckoned them as they left. The only souvenir they took with them to mark the memory was the memory itself.

"Tell us about Israel," their friends and family would say on their return. They'd try. They'd talk about floating in the Dead Sea. About the Mount of Olives and the Garden Tomb. But that other stop? The one not printed in the tour schedule? "I guess you had to be there," they'd finally say.

Because, in their heart, they knew that *that* stop was more than Israel. They knew they'd taken a short detour to the edge of the Great Mystery.

They'd had a glimpse of Love.

CHAPTER 17

Down to the River

Drive a few miles south of the spot the Jordan River exits the Sea of Galilee and take a right. Follow the line of buses down and into the parking lot. You'll find a nice place to visit. A place called Yardenit. They have a *huge* gift shop there. Good deals if you're in the market for jewelry or anything made out of olive wood. When you're done, pass on through the back door, and you'll find yourself standing on the bank of the Jordan. It's a beautiful, picturesque spot. Songs fill the air. Metal-railed, curved walkways lead down to the river, and several sets of stairs continue on to concrete platforms in the water itself. Each walkway, staircase, and platform filled with white-robed pilgrims over the moon for the chance to be baptized in the same river where Jesus and John the Baptist took the biblical dip.

For a fee, you can rent or even buy your own white robe. (White robes are mandatory if you're going into the water.) For a little more you can buy a DVD of your baptismal experience. And you'll always remember the fish nibbling your toes. They're very aggressive, angry little fish. I suspect the Jordan River fish are not saved.

I know I sound facetious. I might be a little. But the truth is, no matter where a believer's baptism happens, it's a special experience. I count it a high honor to have been asked to baptize friends and travelers at Yardenit.

We broke the rules during one visit. I was in the middle of baptizing a few people when a woman who had originally opted not to take the plunge changed her mind and asked me if it was too late. "Of course not," I told her. The next thing I knew, she'd taken a flying leap and landed in the water—clothes, shoes, and all. I don't think we were too popular with the staff, but no one said anything, and the woman glowed, dripping wet, the whole two-hour bus ride back to the hotel.

I saw at least one website that tells you Yardenit is the actual spot of Jesus's baptism. You don't have to be a Bible scholar or a geographer to see they're stretching the truth on that one by about a hundred kilometers. A cursory reading of John's Gospel will tell you that.

We were in the Galilee region about to head south when Big Jim mentioned that Linda, a friend traveling with us, wanted to get baptized in the Jordan.

"Well, there are a couple different options," I said.

"What are they and what's the difference between them?"

"One is pretty, peaceful, and clean. They have a huge gift shop, and everyone gets baptized in white robes. It's very 'O Brother, Where Art Thou.'"

"Okay. What's the other?"

"The other is the more traditional location. If not the exact spot where John baptized Jesus, then definitely close. It's not pretty. It's in the desert. In the West Bank, actually. They closed the area to the public after the Six-Day War in 1967, but it's been reopened since 2011. You have to pass through a military checkpoint and then go down a road between some old minefields. Don't worry. They're fenced off.

Also, it's below the Alumot Dam, so it's a little polluted. And Israeli and Jordanian guards with machine guns watch each other across the river. Sound fun?"

I knew which spot Big Jim would choose. He smiled.

We waved at the road to Yardenit when we passed it.

We drove south, away from the narrow streets of Tiberias and along the western edge of the Sea of Galilee with its parks and hotels, picking up the Jordan, and following it south.

Seventeen miles below the Sea of Galilee, the Jezreel Valley comes in from the west. History is as old as man here. Think Abraham's own Route 66. These valleys have been traversed by travelers and traders for thousands of years. There's future here too. You might have heard the Jezreel Valley referred to by another name—the Valley of Armageddon. Yes, that old prophecy of doom and destruction and war.

You wouldn't have known its dark future by the way the little burg of Beit She'an napped in the morning sun.

Beit She'an National Park is a must if you're bouncing around Israel. It's a glorious ruin, heavy with history. First Chronicles says King Saul's body was impaled on the wall of Beit She'an. Sprawling Roman ruins exist to this day, sure to impress as they pull you back to another era. I usually head to the theater first. It's the best-preserved Roman theater in Samaria. Every time I visit, I'm reminded afresh of the incredible architectural prowess and art of the Roman Empire. A period of building, engineering, and intellect we don't even come close to duplicating in our modern world, even with all our computers, tools, and technology.

Most Israel tours include Beit She'an. It's an impressive site. But due to fast-moving schedules, tours usually bypass the hippodrome, the oval-shaped Ben Hur colosseum once used to entertain the masses with chariot races, gladiators, and—that age-old Roman favorite—killing Christians. The hippodrome is separate from the main portion of the park, and that means another loading and unloading of the bus. The tour guides' decisions are totally understandable.

But if you're on your own, take the time to check your map and hunt it down. It's actually very close. When you find it, you'll most likely have the place to yourself. Don't just look and leave. Climb down inside and really feel it. Let your mind wander back through the centuries. As a Christian, I can't help but wonder what it must have been like to hear thousands of onlookers, drunk and sick on wine and violence, screaming for your blood. Your family's blood. Take a look around.

At the edge of the arena, duck into one of the holding cells. Yes, they're still there. Stop and be still for a few minutes. Listen to the dust hanging in the single shaft of sunlight. Think about the people waiting in that same little room to be tossed off this earth in some violent, elaborate way. Sword, lions, crocodiles. . . . Then imagine a man—a husband and a father—looking into the eyes of his wife and little girl, all three of them knowing what's about to come. He would have known he could stop it, even then. After all, the Romans prided themselves on being modern, on being reasonable. All that the superstitious, crazy Christians had to do was denounce loyalty to that troublemaking *Christus* and swear allegiance to the Roman gods, and they'd be off the hook. They could go home to their families, to their lives.

So imagine the father clinging to his faith, counting his life— and even the lives of his family—as a small price in comparison to the glory that awaits them.

The door swings open. His daughter is ripped from his arms. He begs mercy for her. "She's first" is the reply. Nothing more. The bars offer a perfect view—ground level—even better than the procurator's view from his special box in the stands. The father doesn't want to watch but can't tear his eyes away. Lions—starved for days—are released. They make quick work, but not quick enough. His daughter's screams tangle with his and his wife's. The door opens again. The two are led out onto ground soaked with their daughter's blood.

And the crowds go wild.

But the church went wild too. Unbelievable as it sounds, Jesus's church grew by leaps under the Roman persecution and the brutal deaths of men and women and children, of our brothers and sisters. Hippolytus torn apart by horses. Ignatius of Antioch eaten alive by lions at the Coliseum. Polycarp burned at the stake and then stabbed when the fire didn't kill him. Felicitas, a woman well known for her tireless work sharing the Gospel, was given a chance to recant after each execution of one of her sons—all seven of them. Seven sons, seven opportunities, and seven times she looked to heaven for her comfort. She followed her boys into the arms of the Father—obtaining for herself, as the writer of Hebrews puts it, a *better* resurrection (11:35).

What men meant for evil, God redeemed for good because He *is* good. These saints' unwavering faith and even their joy in the face of a sure and horrible death didn't go unnoticed. Many of those bloodthirsty onlookers were drawn to the truth and goodness of what they'd seen and chose to follow Jesus themselves, inspiring Tertullian to proclaim, "The blood of the martyrs is the seed of the Church."

Death to the Christians—it's a story that has been repeated through the centuries. *Your* story. *My* story. And it's not over. Today, an average 90,000 believers are butchered every year around the world. Their only crime? Reaching out and taking the hand of the God of Mercy and Love. The very Man who taught, "Love your enemies, bless those who curse you, do good to those who hate you, and pray for those who spitefully use you and persecute you" (Matthew 5:44).

Those believers were on my mind one day, years ago. We were leaving the Beit She'an hippodrome, quiet and sober, deep in thought, when I saw Michelle crouch to look at something. I walked over. There, among the litter and ghosts and tumbleweeds, was a flower. Bright yellow and perfect—the only spot of color in the entire place—pushing its way out of the hard-packed dirt. What a beautiful reminder that even in the most terrible darkness, our God will have His way.

He will bring life. And there will be beauty for ashes.

As the morning sun climbed higher, I piled back into the van with Big Jim and company. Our final destination was still several miles south on the Jordan River, but we had time. We could either drive over and see Gideon's famous biblical spring or swim at a nearby oasis. Without hesitation, my friends decided swimming would be the way to go. No problem. The perfect place was only a few kilometers away.

We drove on through the dust of modern Beit She'an and took a backroad west, pushing deeper into the Jezreel Valley to the oasis of Gan HaShlosha.

Gan HaShlosha is pure Israel, one of the most beautiful places in the country. Waterfalls and deep, crystal-clear pools naturally heated to eighty-three degrees year-round. Tours might pull in occasionally, but I've never seen them. No exception that day. Locals only when we parked our van next to the grass bordering the biggest pool. I told the guys to go ahead and swim. I'd stay with the van and all our bags.

I lay back in the grass and closed my eyes. The summer sounds of splashing and laughter. The sun felt good. Hebrew and Arabic banter mixed. Bees buzzed in the tree branches above me. I might have dozed off.

I woke to the aroma of grilling meat. It made my mouth water. Twenty feet or so away, an Arab family sat around a picnic table. A couple of the men manned a grill. One of them noticed me watching and nodded. I told them how good it smelled. More nods. A few minutes later a young girl approached and asked in very good English if I'd like to join them for the meal. I very much would have liked to, but I knew we had to get on the road. I explained, thanking them profusely, knowing what an honor it was for a stranger—especially an obvious Westerner like me—to be invited to a Middle Eastern table. They were offering to share more than just food; they were opening their lives. The invitation rode with me, warmed me, as we drove on.

We retraced part of our route, but skipped the town of Beit She'an by taking Route 669 southwest out through the mouth of the Jezreel. We popped back on to Highway 90 and headed south. A few miles later we hit the military checkpoint letting us know—in no uncertain terms—that we were entering the West Bank.

If you've watched or read the news or have even a cursory knowledge of Israel, you've heard of the West Bank. And I imagine what you've heard isn't good. For good reason. Frankly, the West Bank is a hotbed of Palestinian resistance and violence. A who's who of terrorist organizations operate in the area. Nablus, Hebron, Ramallah—

all places I personally wouldn't visit unless I was with someone who really knew the lay of the land.

The West Bank takes up a large chunk of central Israel, bordered on the east by the "west bank" of the Jordan River. Highway 90 follows the Jordan down. A quiet drive. Ninety is in the West Bank, yes, but it's a road worn thin by constant tour bus travel. It's relatively safe.

Tired from the swim, the group dozed as I drove. The shepherds watching over their flocks on the hills waved as we passed. One kid riding an impossibly small donkey kicked it into high gear and pretended to race us for a few yards, his feet practically dragging the ground. Eventually, we began to see the outskirts of Joshua's Jericho off to the west. Minarets and modern apartment buildings gleamed in the afternoon sun as did the flat-roofed homes that had rebar sticking out of the tops like shoots of iron grass. Visitors to the Middle East often wonder why Arabs seem to pause midconstruction in the home-building process. The fact is, the houses are not unfinished; they're just built in anticipation of another floor being added at some point. Family is important, so generations often live together, and houses grow up instead of out.

A few miles past Jericho's tumbled walls, we came up on a small road sign: Qasr al Yahud. This was it.

We turned left and drove down the narrow road. We stopped at a guard station where a sharp-eyed Israeli soldier inquired about our business. I told him we wanted to see the river, and a couple of us wanted to get baptized. He gave a polite, neutral nod and opened the gate for us.

The road ran straight as an arrow for a while. Signs on wire fences warned of mines on both sides. Wide swaths of absolutely nothing beyond. No problem on my part. I had no intention of going off-roading. After a while the route wound around and then stopped: a bar across the road marked the end for vehicular travel. A few buses were parked on the gravel. Desert heat waves radiated off the asphalt as we walked the short distance that remained.

The site had a couple of rough restrooms and partitions to change behind. I waited while my friends got ready. When they emerged, we walked down the steps to a wide patio area built out of white Jerusalem stone.

Qasr al Yahud attracts a lot of pilgrims of the Catholic and Orthodox bent. The feeling down by the water was serious; the mood, quiet. Definitely not a swimming hole. A group of Ethiopian Orthodox Christians stood together on the platform. Pristine, perfect, 100 percent beautiful. White robes spotless, their gleaming hair intricately braided. They sang as they walked into the water. Such a deep and contagious spirit of reserved joy.

We waited, watching. A moment in time, celebrated by unfamiliar songs of praise. We didn't understand the language, but we thrilled to the Spirit.

Across the narrow river a couple Jordanian soldiers stood guard, guns at the ready. On our side, two Israelis did the same.

The Ethiopians sang on, rejoicing as they emerged.

Big Jim and Linda went in. Muddy water swirled around their legs, then their waists. Jim did the honors. Linda smiled as she came up, water streaming off her hair, melodic Ethiopian music the perfect aural backdrop for the moment.

I wondered what John the Baptist would think if he'd stood there with us. Burned hard by the sun. Hair matted and tangled, wild in the hot wind. From those banks he'd shouted a fierce and wonderful message of repentance that reverberated all the way up to Jerusalem.

All the way to Ethiopia. All the way to Big Jim's North Carolina and my Idaho. And on that muddy shore, in the presence of the Man-God, John had uttered the most earthshaking declaration ever spoken. The perfect and complete doctrine of Truth in one, simple sentence.

"Behold! The Lamb of God who takes away the sin of the world!" (See John 1:29.)

And heaven boomed. "This is My beloved Son, in whom I am well pleased" (Matthew 3:17).

As we started back toward the van, the orange sun dipped low. The same sun that once reflected the translucent feathers of that celestial descending Dove. The same sun that pushed through iron bars and warmed a little Christian family in a cell beneath a Roman arena.

The same sun that lit Linda's face as she rose from the water.

The same sun that would come again tomorrow, finding us far to the south.

A jet left a trail of white overhead. Residual heat radiated from the asphalt.

Life is really a long string of moments. Most forgotten; a few remembered.

I remember that one.

I remember feeling part of something bigger, something eternal, something infinite and good.

As I reached into my pocket for the keys, I paused, turning to look one more time out over the empty nothing. The desert wind gusted, tugging my clothes. Snatching up Ethiopian songs and swirling them out over the minefields.

CHAPTER 18

Paper Prayers

My first trip to Israel was with Bill Perkins and Compass International. I like Bill. He's generous, he's a walking Bible commentary, and—my favorite part—he has this super-smooth southern accent that makes you want to sit on a front-porch swing sipping ice-cold lemonade or sweet tea.

Bill likes to spring surprises. Just to keep life interesting, he says things like "Hey, Buck, I'm glad y'all are in Egypt. You're gonna be a bus captain! Just follow the guy with the machine gun." Or "Hey, Buck, isn't Corinth cool? By the way, you're gonna teach today. Do somethin' good. You know, like on grace. Okay, go ahead."

Thanks to one of Bill's Alabama surprises, I found myself reading the apostle Paul's Mars Hill sermon to a group of travelers as we all stood *on* Mars Hill in Athens, Greece:

"Then Paul stood in the midst of the Areopagus and said, 'Men of Athens, I perceive that in all things you are very religious'" (Acts 17:22).

It was a powerful moment for me, reading Paul's words about the Lord of heaven and earth not dwelling in any temple built by human hands. And doing so as I stood in the shadow of the Parthenon, that awesome architectural feat built, yes, by human hands in honor of the goddess Athena.

Later that night Michelle and I climbed the stairs to the roof of our hotel and looked across Athens at the Acropolis. The Parthenon's pillars shone bright in the spotlights, a monument to human greatness. Really beautiful. Really impressive.

Really empty.

Very religious, Paul said. I guess we're all—Protestant, Catholic, Muslim, New Age—guilty of that in our own way. I have atheist friends just as passionate about spreading their gospel of hopelessness as the soapbox-Pentecostal fire-and-brimstoning folks on the street corners.

In Paul's day the Greeks found a million and one things to worship. Whether we admit it or not, we're no different today. We worship sports stars, actors, singers. Anybody or anything famous. Doesn't matter how they got that way. We worship relationships. We worship toys. We worship sex. We like to worship pastors. And some of them bow in humility—or not—loving to be worshipped.

We worship kids and Kardashians.

We worship Donkeys and Elephants.

We worship church, and we even worship *worship.*

Something that always surprises me is how many people seem to worship Israel. I remember my first trip. I was humbled to be invited, but I wasn't sure what to expect. Everyone I'd met who'd been there painted it as the ultimate mountaintop experience. "You'll feel like you've come home," they said. "You'll *never* feel safer than you do when you're in Israel." You've probably heard that too. One of

Israel's great tourism catchphrases. And maybe people *do* feel safer. Maybe you've been there and felt that way yourself.

I didn't.

On the bus ride from Ben Gurion Airport to our first hotel, I remember a guy doing the chair-to-chair shuffle down the aisle on his way to the restroom, a big grin on his face.

He stopped at my seat. "As soon as I stepped off the plane, I felt like I was home! Didn't you feel home?"

He kept on walking, which saved me either a lie or a longer conversation because when I looked out the window and saw the green lights of minarets dotting the dark landscape, I felt a long, long way from my own bed.

"Yes! And I've never felt this safe!" a woman across the aisle chimed in.

I'm glad she felt safe. I thought about feeling safe myself. If I'm being honest—and I want to be—I didn't feel *not* safe. I think I was neutral on that one. But, even at neutral, I'd probably have felt a little bit safer sitting next to my barbecue on the back patio of my old farmhouse back in Idaho. I felt bad for not feeling *more*. Or not feeling *better* about the whole deal. Maybe I needed to try harder to be a better *feeler* all around.

The thing is, as much hate and anti-Semitism as there is in the world, especially toward the nation of Israel proper, there's a definite flip side of the coin—the Israel junkies. I think Israel worship makes them feel spiritual (as if *spiritual* is something you can feel). So they worship earth and stone and coordinates on a map. Politics and posturing. They venerate the Jewish people as if they weren't sinners like everyone else. Like Madonna or Billy Graham or John the Baptist.

A handful of theologians out there even preach a dual covenant: the Jews don't need Jesus Christ as Messiah because they are uniquely rescued through the Abrahamic Covenant. I know Messianic Jews who grieve over this and consider the doctrine of a dual covenant the greatest act of hatred and violence against Jews since the Holocaust. I think of Mars Hill Paul, willing to burn in hell if only his countrymen might be saved.

In short, we too often worship the creation rather than the Creator. We love our golden calves. I love the Jewish people, and I love Israel. But I'm very, very careful where I direct my worship.

There's an interesting—and spiritually disturbing—phenomenon called the Jerusalem Syndrome. It blows my mind every time I hear about it. Dozens of times a year, tourists—mostly evangelical Protestants—are so overwhelmed by the Israel experience they just melt down. Sometimes crying, sometimes shouting spiritual messages, sometimes—I'm not kidding—stripping the sheet from the hotel bed and wandering out into the desert prophesying gibberish to the rocks and sky. Ask any Israeli tour guide. They all have stories. In fact, there are medical experts in Israel who actually specialize in studying and dealing with Jerusalem Syndrome patients.

Please don't misunderstand. I fully believe God meets people in Israel. I know He's met me time and time again. Stop in and talk to Moshe—a devout member of Jerusalem's Religious Zionist community—at the Shorashim Biblical Shop in the Jewish Quarter. He loves to tell you, "If you're here, you've been invited by God." It's true. I never discount God's work. But it's *God's* work, not Israel's work. Be careful not to mix up the two.

It comes down to this: we all step out of our mother's womb wanting. Striving to fill the void in our lives. We feel it in our bellies first. It's milk we want. But we move quickly on to other things. Eventually we realize the physical isn't enough. We crave the spiritual. A thousand distractions press in, a million different roads we can take. We chant, meditate, go to church, count rosary beads, serve in soup kitchens, walk across India—the list is endless and as old as man.

What we actually hunger for is God. And sometimes we find Him. Or He finds us.

Because, the beautiful thing is, He hungers too.

Whether we are Jew or Gentile, the answer is Jesus, but too often Jesus is relegated to a vague theory in the third verse of a worship song. So, in the Christian ghetto, seekers sometimes drift. Sometimes they find other seekers—other bits of flotsam and jetsam on that murky religious sea—and start home churches, hoping to get back to the original *way*. Others look into mysticism or a liturgical experience.

And many look for spiritual answers and fulfillment in Israel or some sect of Judaism.

Madonna plays with Kabbalah, Jewish mysticism. Whitney Houston found her home among the Black Hebrew Israelites in the Negev Desert. I know Gentiles who've searched through family trees with a fine-tooth comb to find any hint of Jewish heritage. Whether they find it or not, they're suddenly wearing yarmulkes on their heads, hanging tzitzits from their clothes, and struggling to hold up under an Old Covenant law no man or woman can bear.

A few days into that first trip, we walked down the series of stairs leading from the Jewish Square in the Old City. Our destination: the Western Wall, considered the holiest place on earth for Jews to pray. My first time there, but I'd heard the stories. This was *the* place to encounter God. As we turned a corner, I paused and listened to an American tourist leading an Israeli man in the sinner's prayer. The

Israeli's clothes were ragged; his face, gaunt. He hung his head and wiped a tear. A little farther on, a cluster of old women, scarfs tied tight under their chins, chattered at me and tried to tie red Kabbalah strings on my wrists. "Sure to ward off the evil eye!" they said. Con games weren't new to me. I made it through the Kabbalah gauntlet, shekels intact and red thread–less.

We passed through the heavy security gate into the Western Wall courtyard. The men and women in our group separated, men to the left, women to the right. I passed the fenced entry to the men's area. I had a hat on, so I didn't need one of the cardboard ones provided. I moved up to the wall itself. Huge stones, bigger and taller than I'd expected. Tiny folded pieces of paper—a million prayers—were stuffed into every crack, nook, and cranny. I put my hand against the wall. The evening held a chill, but the stone was still warm from the day. To my right, a soldier leaned his forehead against the smooth surface, eyes closed, not speaking. To my left, several Haredim men bobbed back and forth and read monotone prayers from small books. I bowed my head and closed my eyes.

Someone touched my arm. An Orthodox man. For a little cash he'd help me pray.

"No, thank you. I'm okay on my own," I told him.

He asked again, insistent this time. Pushing. He held a stiff hand out.

We went back and forth a few times before, with an exasperated shake of his head, he moved on to someone else.

I prayed for a few minutes. Prayed for safety, prayed for my family, thanked God for life and breath. More men on either side of me now. More bobbing. More murmured prayers bouncing off the stone. I saw a fellow traveler from my group praying, crying, clearly moved.

Was this it? The great spiritual experience I'd heard so much about? I did an internal search. No rapture or euphoria. All I really felt was sad for the black-hatted bobbers. They came across as desperate, like drowning men.

I looked again at all the tiny prayers. "Lord, are You here?"

"Of course."

"I'm supposed to feel something great, but all I feel is sad." It was true. A deep, deep sadness. No mountaintops. No clouds of glory. Just that sadness. The place seemed the ultimate pinnacle of religious posturing. Mankind, insisting on keeping his eyes squeezed shut, banging his throbbing head against the wall, while Unimaginable Love waited and wept, arms open, right next to him.

"They grope for me in the darkness. . . ."

Reciting Acts 17:27, I'd read those words to the sky and wind on Mars Hill not a week before, how people seeking the Lord may find Him.

"They grope for You in the darkness."

"Yet I am not far from them. . . ."

"I don't want to wonder. I don't even want to hope. I want to *know.* I want to be with You."

"You are with Me. And I'm with you. And it will never end."

"I'm supposed to feel at home here, but I don't think I do."

"You'll feel at home when you're home. Home with Me. Not before."

I looked down the wall again. Bobbing, reciting . . . *groping.* They broke my heart. I wanted to tell them. I wanted them to understand—*He's right here.*

There's no blanket, one-size-fits-all God experience. He is real, and He is His own. He has a personality and a will outside of ours. He meets us where we are. He draws, He loves, He shares Himself with us.

As we walked back up the stairs, Temple Mount behind us, people talked about how moved they'd been at the Wall. They smiled, chatted, and shared their stories. I was glad for them. I'd been moved too. We'd spoken there, He and I. I'd known His voice.

But I'd also know Him later at the hotel.

And, after that, back in Idaho or wherever the Spirit might take me. The same familiar voice, the same constant presence, the same arm around my shoulder I'd felt all my life.

An old woman held a red string out to me. I smiled and shook my head no. A little farther on the same raggedy Israeli man was saying another sinner's prayer, a different tourist this time. Hey, man, I guess you can never be too sure. People took pictures and videos with their cell phones. A man in the business of getting saved. As I passed, the happy evangelist pulled out his wallet to give the guy a little something. There'd be groceries on the table tonight.

I thought about Jesus's words: "O Jerusalem, Jerusalem, the one who kills the prophets and stones those who are sent to her! How often I wanted to gather your children together, as a hen gathers her chicks under her wings, but you were not willing!" (Matthew 23:37). I knew that, above and among those noisy streets, God still *desired*. He still hovered and moved over the deep, loving the old women hawking their evil-eye insurance, loving the wide-eyed, safe-feeling tourists, loving the raggedy grifter.

God was still loving the world, still waiting for people to come home.

I asked the tour guide what happened to all those tiny prayers stuffed into those cracks between the stones. Did they throw them away? Did they save them? No, he told me, a couple times a year the rabbis take out the papers, put them into bags, and bury them in the cemetery on the Mount of Olives.

"Do they read them first?"

"No, they're personal. No one ever reads them."

That's not true, I thought. *Someone reads them.* When He does, He laughs, weeps, and stores our tears in a bottle. And here, in the darkness on the edge of the light, He is not far from us.

CHAPTER 19

A Season of Constant Unbalance

I watched the world come loose through a hotel window in Omaha, Nebraska. Must have been close to midnight, but lightning turned the streets and buildings into high noon. Thunder shook the floor and walls. Then the rain. I crawled into bed to the sound of Niagara Falls pounding my barrel.

Welcome to the Midwest.

I played the next morning at a pastor's conference, with sunlight—washed clean by the storm—pushing through stained glass. One of those old church buildings you still find in middle America. Lots of brick and wood. A century's worth of hymns soaked into the walls. Stuff you can't cover with primer and paint. It was good being there, part of God's family. I listened and watched as pastors from around the region took turns giving reports on their local church programs, struggles, and progress.

It went on for a while. Good guys. Faithful to their calling. A man took the stage as another stepped off. An unassuming-looking man. His humble manner struck me right off the bat. He stood for a while, like maybe he needed to collect his thoughts, and took in the room. When he spoke, he wasn't loud, but I found myself listening closely.

"Hi, I'm Dennis," he said. "I came out here from California to plant our church in 1999. We've worked very hard these years. We thought it would grow fast." He looked around the room again. "Today, after all our efforts, our congregation numbers about twenty people."

I glanced around the room. Everyone was watching. Quiet.

Most don't say it out loud, but—like it or not—in Western church culture, success is most often measured by numerical growth. Not a biblical concept. In fact, not even close. As far as I can tell, the New Testament church measured success in *spiritual* growth—in maturity, love, and joy. *God* did the building.

Today seminars are held, countless books are written, programs are developed—all designed to fill seats so a house of worship can be "successful."

Which can make it very hard for a man like Dennis—faithfully ministering for years to the handful of souls God placed before him— to stand in front of a room full of pastors and not feel like a failure.

Dennis offered a nervous smile. "Only twenty people, but if it's okay, I'd like to take a few minutes to tell you about them. . . ."

Then he did something surprising and (I think) a little wonderful: he went on to talk about each and every one of his parishioners. He went through them name by name. He talked of their struggles and joys. I saw pride on his face when he talked of a young girl who dreamed of serving on the mission field. Marriages, jobs, schools, sicknesses, accomplishments—sometimes he laughed. At other points he teared up.

When he was done, he said a simple thanks and walked off. I was stunned. I wanted everyone to cheer. To recognize the fact we'd been blessed to listen to a man who simply loved the people God had charged him with. An obedient man. Here was a *pastor*, a shepherd. Exemplifying the heart of our *Great* Shepherd in living Technicolor. Meeting and loving the *one*, just as Jesus did.

I made it a point to sit with Dennis at dinner. I asked him if I could come to his church sometime when I was in the area again. I wanted to meet those twenty people of his. Maybe God could even use me to minister to them, to minister to Dennis. He was happy to say yes.

A couple years later I had the opportunity. Lincoln, Nebraska. I sat on a stool with my guitar and hung out with those in the room, doing my best to share the heart of Jesus. Afterward, Dennis and I found a late-night café. As I sipped my coffee, I told him how much that day at the pastor's conference had moved me.

His eyes moistened. "Can I tell you something? I feel like I'm in a season of constant unbalance. I don't know when it will end, but I've learned—at least I think I've learned—it's where I'm supposed to be."

We talked a long time that night. I made a new friend. The next morning he met me out in front of the motel. We said our goodbyes, and I headed down the road.

A season of constant unbalance. I couldn't get that phrase out of my head, and I couldn't have said it better. I'd seen a lot of miles. I've seen a lot more since. And I've honestly still never quite found my footing. Years have been a persistent teacher, and Dennis put a title to the lesson.

Mile after mile God has worked cheerfully in my discomposure. I've seen it more times than I can count. He laughs and loves and invites me along for the ride, asking me only to remember I'm not the one driving the bus. His will exists outside of mine, no doubt. Maybe that's what faith is: simply closing our eyes and hanging on. I hope so. Because that's all I've got.

No cloud broke the Nebraska blue as I left the city. Through my windshield the lined strip of asphalt slashed straight as an arrow through the cornfields. I wasn't sure what that road would bring. But then again, I didn't need to know.

Constant unbalance. . . .

Israel has one of the best road signs in the world: a big triangle with nothing but an exclamation point on it. I think when you see it on the driver's test, the answer is C—as in "Oh crap!" Driving in Israel isn't exactly like driving in India or Egypt. It's not a *complete* wild and woolly free-for-all. Still, it's fast, aggressive, and it can get intense.

I settled in without much problem the first time I drove there. I turned on my Elvis GPS, put the van in gear, pulled anchor, and hoisted the sails. Seas were calm with a fair wind off the beam. My group and I spent a nice morning exploring Caesarea Maritima. The Mediterranean, a gentle blue-green, lapped the shore. We climbed down the rocks and walked the ruins of Herod the Great's freshwater swimming pool, imagining the palace in its glory days jutting out into the remnants of a harbor once considered one of the wonders of the ancient world. Then we climbed back up and stood on the spot the apostle Paul made his case before Governor Felix. We walked the massive amphitheater (still in use today) and the hippodrome.

We had lunch in the ruins at one of my favorite falafel joints on the planet and then pointed our dented bow north. We made good time, straight up Highway 2 hugging the Mediterranean coast. GPS

Elvis and I had a clear understanding, and we both agreed our destination was Tiberias. Elvis's job was simple: tell me when to turn east on Highway 65. Teamwork. Just a simple matter of communication.

Elvis must have dozed off. Then again there's also the slightest chance I wasn't listening. Either way, Highway 65 came and went. I didn't even realize it until mountains grew high to the starboard, and the port landscape morphed from beach-vacation to shipyard-urban. Buildings grew, and I started to suspect I'd accidentally found Haifa. I tried to check with Elvis, but he had no input on the matter at all. He'd left the building. I had nothing but a blank cell phone screen. So much for our partnership. No question, I was lost.

I had crashed headlong into a season of serious unbalance.

I'd been to Haifa a time or two, but I'd never been driving. To say I didn't know my way around would be an understatement. The trusty paper map showed a road cutting east out of the city, but all I saw in that direction was the steep face of Mount Carmel. Oh, well, Elvis might be gone, but maps don't lie, right? I turned east.

Did you know there's an eight-kilometer tunnel that cuts under Mount Carmel?

Neither did I.

I do now.

I also didn't know it was a toll road—with signs all in Hebrew. I had no idea what I was doing. I looked for a place to turn around. *Nada.* The traffic-tide pushed us forward, and the mountain swallowed our little ship like Pinocchio's whale. Day turned to night, and I suddenly found myself racing some weird, underground grand prix. Sound booming through the tunnel as if somewhere far above fire still rained down from heaven and Elijah taunted the priests of Ba'al.

Engines roared. Horns honked. Racers jockeyed for position. I glanced at Elvis, but he was still passed out cold.

The road split, offering two options. And Hebrew signs. I took one. Maybe a bus lane, maybe taxis-only. Who knew? Maybe I was in for some astronomical fine. Or Israeli prison. I had no idea. Eventually we came up to a kiosk. The man inside scowled and growled out a sentence—in Hebrew, of course. I asked him if he spoke English. He repeated whatever he'd said, sounding even more Hebrew-ish than before if there could even be such a thing. The car behind me honked, then another, then a whole angry bleating chorus. The man spoke again, and I thought I caught the word *shekels* in the barrage. I abandoned the communication effort, grabbed everything in my pocket, and handed it over. The man rolled his eyes and picked through the money. He handed some back and waved me on with an angry hand.

Eight kilometers . . . I held a hand up to the harsh sunlight. Elvis blinked and then deigned to bless us with his presence again. Mount Carmel filled the rearview mirror. Thankfully, it didn't take long to figure out a route to Tiberias from where we were.

We drove through a couple towns. The road split, divided by a median. Cars and trucks flew along, passing, being passed, zooming— the projector switched to fast-forward. I saw lights flashing up ahead, heard sirens. Red brake lights, traffic slowed. An accident, surely. I hoped it wasn't bad.

It was more than bad.

A bus had rear-ended a tractor-trailer truck hard enough to accordion the trailer and knock the entire rig off the road. The bus's shattered windshield hung from its seal, and the driver slumped across the wheel. I couldn't see what had happened to all the people inside.

The ones I could see weren't moving. Soldiers spilled out of a truck in front of us. One began directing traffic while others sprinted toward the accident. I prayed for all of them as my season of constant unbalance shaped into an internal storm of flat-out stress.

It wasn't much farther to Tiberias. We took a left-hand turn partway down the grade dropping into the city. I wanted to drive up to the top of Mount Arbel before heading for the Beit Bracha Guest House, our base camp for a few days. The two-lane road to the top of Arbel meandered and wound through fields and low grassland. Such a peaceful place, and I tried my best to let some of it soak into my shaken bones. Bit by bit I started to relax. Up ahead a farmer poked along on an ancient tractor. I slowed. I couldn't see around him, and I wanted to make sure I was clear to pass.

And then I heard tires shriek.

My eyes shot to the rearview, and my heart went to my throat. It all happened in half a second. White smoke from burning tires blew out from beneath a car barreling down on us. I saw the driver clearly in my rearview mirror, his mouth open in a scream as his car started to fishtail. No way he could miss us, and I braced for impact.

It never came.

The car, tires still locked and squealing, blew by on my left not six inches from the driver's-side door. To this day I believe it was a miracle he didn't hit us. I can't explain it any other way.

The road straightened, and I passed the tractor. The other car shrank in the distance, far up the road.

A mile later we took a couple turns, skirted a kibbutz, and drove up the mountain. We parked in the lot and hiked the easy fifteen minutes to the top. Across the Galilee a thin haze hung over the green hills of the Golan Heights. Out of the precipice a hawk swung wide, lazy circles, in no hurry. I drew in a long breath and then slowly let it out, thanking the Lord for sparing us serious injury.

We had dinner at Beit Bracha. Afterward, people drifted off to the patio or down to the garden. Lights across the lake traced shimmery pathways on the water. A piano tinkled, and someone sang. So much peace in that place, but I couldn't shake the day no matter how hard I tried. I decided to turn in. *After all, it was over,* I told myself. *Let the day fade in the rearview mirror like Mount Carmel.* I pulled the news up on my phone as I lay in bed. Not a good idea. Top story: an imam in Iran calling terrorists everywhere to kidnap Americans. To drive a stake through the heart of the Great Satan.

Perfect. The next day we were driving through the West Bank.

Constant unbalance. . . .

I knew we were in the Lord's hands. I believed it in my mind, but in that moment and in that place, I couldn't convince my heart. I prayed. It didn't help. I sought God. I asked Him to speak, to comfort. Sleep wouldn't come. I tossed, turned, then tossed some more.

Lying there, I recognized how my discomfort and stress—my season of constant unbalance—had, at that point, become unreasonable. It had crossed the line from a physical, fleshly situation to being a full-on spiritual attack. Dark water rose, and I was drowning.

Then God threw me a line: I had a dream. . . .

I found myself standing outside the Dung Gate of the Old City. People pushed and shoved. Horns blared. Chaos all around me. I put my hands over my ears as my heart tried its best to pound its way out of my body

A taxi pulled to the curb and stopped. The driver got out. Other cars honked, irate commuters leaning out, shouting for him to move the car. The driver ignored them all. Instead, he walked straight to me. He was short. His head barely came to my shoulder. Middle-aged, Jewish, nondescript. He had dark hair and wore wire-rimmed glasses. I remember he had on brown polyester pants and a striped shirt.

And in my dream I knew he was Jesus.

I don't know how, but I *knew*. He put his arms around me and pulled me to him. Pulled my head down to his shoulder.

He spoke quietly in my ear. I can still hear the words: "You're My child. I'll let nothing happen to you."

That was it. Nothing more. I woke with a start. Dim orange light from the patio filtered through the window. I heard the fountain outside bubbling. And, I tell you, I'd never felt such joyous, overwhelming, wide-awake peace. I lay in the dark, clinging to the moment.

To this day I look back on that night—that dream—as one of my life's turning points. It hasn't always been smooth sailing, and the feeling of *constant unbalance* is still part of the journey. But, like my friend Dennis, I've learned it's a place I need to be. I don't always know what God is doing, but I don't need to. He's God, and I'm not. He's wild, He's free, He's not bound by my will or that of *any* man.

It's enough for me.

Why a taxi driver? I have no idea. Why Jerusalem? Why the Dung Gate? No clue. But I know what I'd suffered that night was real. And I know my God, with nothing more than a whisper— a thought—blew away my anxiety, my faithlessness, my dark attackers like they were nothing.

I walked in confidence and faith the rest of that trip. Little miracles marked our passing.

I've never forgotten.

And His arms are still around me.

CHAPTER 20

Confession Is Good for the Soul

I can prove the existence of God by the people
He puts next to me on airplanes.

DAVE HUNT

In your eyes, I see the doorway to a thousand churches.

PETER GABRIEL

That's some pretty deep stuff, man.

ME

I dropped into my seat, beat to the core. It'd been a long trip, and I was ready to see the lights of Tel Aviv behind me and the good ol' US of A in front of me. I wanted my wife, my bed, my back porch, my barbecue, something cold to drink, and no wake-up call for a few hundred mornings. And I wanted to sleep till I got there.

I watched a smiling Hispanic woman coming down the aisle of the plane, chatting away with her fellow travelers. And I knew—the way you always know on a crowded airplane—that this over-exuberant bundle of cheerfulness would be in the seat next to me.

Don't judge me. You've been there too.

What to do? The standard feign sleep trick? Pull out a book? Too late to strategize. She flopped down next to me and flashed a grin. I tried to return the expression, but I imagine the finished product looked more like the Grinch than a smile. (I've never been a good poker player.)

"Were you visiting Israel?" Hispanic Pollyanna asked.

We were still sitting on the runway in Tel Aviv, and so many junior-high responses jumped into my mind I had to beat them back with a stick. I opted for "Uh-huh, sure was."

"Did you love it?"

Her little legs didn't reach the floor, and she swung them back and forth. This irritated me since my knees are usually somewhere tucked around my ears on commercial flights. "Yes. I loved it." *How hard would it be to reach my book?*

"I came with Father John!"

Now, I had no idea who Father John was, but at the moment he wasn't high on my list of favorite people. "Oh? Good."

"He's my priest," she said.

"I figured that."

"Did you love the Church of the Holy Sepulchre?"

"Um, I didn't actually go there."

"What? You have to go! Father John told us it's where Holy Jesus was crucified and buried. I'm telling you, *mijo*, I met God there!"

I thought about telling her I'd been there before. It really *is* an incredible place. Then I thought about arguing Father John's archaeological veracity. Then God slapped me on the back of the head. He likes to do that when I'm being a jerk.

"What?" I said to Him.

"*I love her.*"

"And who the heck is Father John?"

"*I love him too.*"

"She's not gonna stop talking. I can tell."

"*She's excited.*"

"And then she says she met You at the Church of the Holy Sepulchre."

"*How do you know she didn't?*"

He had a good point—but, then again, when didn't He?

My new travel mate still smiled up at me. This time I think I actually managed to smile back. "Okay," I said, "tell me about meeting God."

So she did.

We talked. A half hour later I realized I loved her, too, short legs and all.

As she chatted on . . . and on . . . I thought back to *my* first Israel experience. The first site I visited on that very first trip was the Mount of Beatitudes. The Sermon on the Mount—an event that takes up three chapters of the Bible. Five loaves and a couple fish turned into a party. Heady stuff. Our tour bus had chugged out of Tiberias and edged up the northwest shore of the Sea of Galilee under a gray sky spitting rain. We turned off the road and approached a beautiful building topped with a tall, green patinaed dome. The entrance gate loomed on the left, but we passed it.

"What's the building?" I asked.

"The Church of the Beatitudes. It's Catholic. We don't go there" came the very Protestant reply.

With a hiss of air brakes, the bus came to a stop at the end of a muddy road. The tour guide stood and gave us the long-version historical lowdown. The traditional site of Jesus's sermon, the tremendous acoustics, and the Byzantine chapels—fourth-century and older—that had been found around the site. I listened, but I mostly wanted off the bus. I wanted to stand where Jesus had stood. Where He had taught and lived and performed miracles. I couldn't wait. Finally the bus door opened, and we filed off.

Wikipedia will tell you all about the Church of the Beatitudes. It will tell you about its octagonal floor plan representing the eight Beatitudes. About the rock-cut cistern beneath it and even how a pope or two has celebrated mass there. What Wikipedia *won't* tell you about is the guy who used to have a little olive oil stand on the road outside the gate. Even Google is mum about that one. But the olive oil guy was there that first day. And as we filed off the bus, several people decided to bypass the mount itself and head to the stand instead. I couldn't believe it. Here we were, in a place where you could look out and see where Jesus did most of His ministry, and the first thing on everyone's mind was a good deal on olive oil?

I stood in the rain and looked down the hill. *This was the place!* Three whole chapters . . . yet only a handful of my fellow travelers seemed to care. A million emotions rushed in, none of them good. Mad topped the list. Mad at tourists. Mad at the guide. Mad at the olive oil guy I'd never even met. *How could they not care? How could they not even walk over and look? Loaves and fish! Words of God Himself still echoing across the hills!*

For God so loved the world. . . . If that was the case, then these tourists and the olive oil guy must have been from Mars or Venus or Krypton. Definitely not part of *my* world.

Sometimes indignant irritation just feels so good.

Catholic tours usually opt for the Church of the Beatitudes, but Martin Luther's kids do the hill. They walk down a dirt path next to a banana grove while the bus circles around to pick them up at the bottom. That day the rain had made the path too slick to walk, so we looked out toward Galilee for a few minutes and then started back, some for the bus but most to the olive oil guy's stand. I sat on the bus and waited. No olive oil for me, thanks.

The land of Jesus. . . . The bus rumbled to life and, even though riding low, weighed down with olive oil, managed to tool down the hill. Within spitting distance of the Mount of Beatitudes, you can walk the ruins of the towns Jesus ministered in, taught in, and ultimately cursed—Bethsaida, Chorazin, and Capernaum, all uninhabited to this day.

We parked in the Capernaum lot. Capernaum is a fantastic site to visit. In that little village on the shore of Galilee, Jesus spent most of His adult life, recruited His first disciples, and became known for His miracles. The site boasts two of the oldest synagogues in the world, one built on top of the other. It was here Jesus healed a man's withered hand and was called out by the Pharisees for doing it on the Sabbath. Just outside the synagogue we looked down on an ancient residential neighborhood, still fairly intact. Tradition dating back to the first century points out one of the structures as being the home of Peter, which the New Testament suggests was where Jesus stayed during His time in Capernaum. In the fourth century an octagon-shaped Byzantine church was built on the site of Peter's home. These days a Catholic shrine, shaped to mimic the Byzantine structure, hovers above the site on thick, concrete legs like some flying saucer from a 1950s comic book.

"*What's the matter?*" He asked.

"They built a church over Peter's house."

"*So?*"

"And I'm still torqued at the olive oil guy." Might as well be honest. Not like I could hide anything from Him.

"*Why?*"

"Pulling people from a place where You taught in order to make a buck? Who would do that?"

"*Do you know his name?*"

"No."

"*I do.*"

I looked out across those narrow streets, reminded in mind and spirit of a scene played out there two thousand years ago. A day Jesus rushed along with a father. A man whose daughter lay suffering on death's doorstep.

But then Jesus stopped and turned. Someone had touched Him, and He asked who it had been.

"In this crowd, who *didn't* touch you?" came the reply.

But a woman stood there. Small. Broken. Sick. An outcast, loathed, no better than a dog to the other people crowding around Jesus that day.

But precious to Him.

The crowd looked on in stunned surprise as the God of the universe bent down and asked the woman's story. And then listened . . . to the *entire* story of that fractured soul. Jesus didn't rush her. He didn't stress. He simply loved. And when it was over, the woman left Him. Full and whole—restored.

Jesus. The lover of the *one*.

Years passed after that first trip of mine. Other visits came and went. Then, one day, at the Mount of Beatitudes again, I noticed the olive oil guy was no longer there. I asked about him.

"That guy? I think he died last year," someone said.

I've thought about it a lot since. That younger me, fresh off the plane, standing in the rain, righteous and proud in all my imagined spiritual maturity. Standing quite possibly on the very spot my Jesus taught grace and mercy. The same Jesus who stopped in the street for the filthy and despised. To listen and love and heal. Jesus, who lay down on a cross and spread His arms to die for a faithless world. Who died for me.

Jesus, who knew the olive oil guy's name.

It wasn't about that *place* at all. As amazing as they are, it's never about the shrines or the ruins or the sites. After all, they're mortar, stone, and dust.

Spirit is eternal.

For God, it's about the woman in the street. Always has been. And it's always been about the olive oil guy. The one I never even said hello to. The one I just drove by.

I am ashamed.

And it's also about the little Mexican chatterbox swinging her legs back and forth in the airplane seat next to me. She says she met God. I believe her. Because—at the Church of the Holy Sepulchre, the Garden Tomb, or Krispy Kreme Doughnuts—God will have it no other way.

Turns out, Jesus is bigger than Martin Luther. Bigger than the Pope. Bigger than Father John.

And *definitely* bigger than me.

CHAPTER 21

O'Toole Doesn't Sound Like a Roman Name

Michelle and I love yard sales, garage sales, flea markets—anyplace we can find old stuff. And a bargain. The places are riddled with stories. I usually leave with stacks of books. On occasion I've found a nice vintage guitar or two. One man's junk. . . .

A few months ago we saw a sign for an estate sale at a big old Tudor down the road from us. We were moths to the flame. We walked in through the garage. Lots of tools and some mismatched furniture. Racks and racks of '70s clothes inside. Paintings, more furniture, knickknacks of every sort. I climbed the stairs and found an office. Apparently, the man who'd lived there had been a screenwriter. There were boxes and piles of scripts. Immediately interested, I rummaged through them. A stack of *M*A*S*H* episodes caught my eye. I leafed through looking for familiar scenes.

Near the bottom of the stack, I hit a script that brought me up short. *You've got to be kidding me!* But there it was. The original director's script for the miniseries *Masada* with Peter O'Toole and Barbara Carrera. I opened the first page.

MASADA

Written by
Joel Oliansky

From the novel
The Antagonists
by Ernest K. Gann

A few more pages in, I began to see, in red ink, handwritten notes in the margins. I asked the woman running the sale if she knew anything about it. All she'd heard was that it had been the director's script used on location during filming.

That would be the Masada Plateau overlooking the Dead Sea on the edge of the Judean Desert. A place I knew well. A place I loved.

I hesitated to ask my next question. "What will you take for it?" No doubt the original *Masada* director's script would be a long way above my budget of whatever happened to be in my pocket at the moment.

She gave it a critical, appraising eye and said, "How about twenty bucks?"

Sold. Even though I had to borrow two or three dollars from Michelle to swing it.

From a distance Masada looks like any other mountain in the hard Judean landscape. Brown, desolate, nothing special. Get a little closer and it's a different story. Sheer cliffs, ranging in height from 300 to 1,300 feet, fall away on every side. The top of the mountain is a flat, roughly rhomboid shape 1,800 by 890 feet—a big *defensible* area. Between 37 and 31 BC Herod the Great built palaces for himself there and fortified the summit. Herod wasn't dubbed "the Great" by accident. For all his faults—and they were legion—his building projects lived up to his nickname, and during his life Herodian architecture ruled the day. He built multiple palaces of massive and imaginative scope. Caesarea Maritima and its wonders-of-the-world harbor, Herodium with its four seven-story towers, the amazing reconstructed Temple in Jerusalem—the list is long and impressive. The guy didn't do anything small, and Masada was no exception. He managed to engineer and build a luxury resort in the middle of one of the harshest deserts on the planet, on top of an inaccessible, waterless mountain, complete with barracks, an armory, bathhouses, steam room, pools . . . all the comforts of home. And for Herod, "comforts of home" demanded nothing short of larger-than-life.

But for all his accomplishments, including Masada, Herod the Great didn't have a starring role in my new dog-eared script. The story picks up thirty-five miles north, as the crow flies, in nighttime Jerusalem. On page one—70 AD—the decisive battle of the Jewish-Roman War is underway across the city. A Jewish rebel named Eleazar struggles to flee the city to protect his family.

The events that happened on and around Masada are detailed in the writings of Jewish historian Flavius Josephus. (I think of Josephus as an ancient-day Tom Clancy.) His account offers an epic battle of wills: Roman General Lucius Flavius Silva with an army of eight to nine thousand fighting men against 960 Jewish rebel holdouts led by tenacious Eleazar ben Ya'ir (Peter O'Toole versus Peter Strauss in my estate-sale version). Eleazar and his band held out on the mountain against a three-year Roman siege. Finally, in an amazing military and engineering feat Herod would have admired, the Romans breached the walls by building a massive earthen ramp and rolling a huge battering ram to the top. The rebels determined to die free, by their own hand, rather than submit their families to a lifetime of slavery under the Romans.

Eleazar spoke to his men, his words later relayed to Josephus by two women who survived the ordeal by hiding in a cistern and claimed to remember the words verbatim:

> Since we long ago resolved never to be servants to the Romans, nor to any other than to God Himself, who alone is the true and just Lord of mankind, the time is now come that obliges us to make that resolution true in practice. . . . We were the very first that revolted, and we are the last to fight against them; and I cannot but esteem it as a favor that God has granted us, that it is still in our power to die bravely, and in a state of freedom.

But there was a snag. Jewish law strictly forbids suicide. So the rebels killed their families first and then drew lots, killing each other down to the last man. And that last man, holder of the short straw—or, in this case, shard of pottery—took his own life.

Josephus explained: "Having chosen by lot ten of their number to dispatch the rest . . . these, having unswervingly slaughtered all, ordained the same rule of the lot for one another, that he on whom it fell should slay first the nine and them himself last of all."

An amazing story.

Even more amazing, several shards of pottery have been found on the mountain. Eleven inscribed with names. One name—Ben Yair—points to Eleazar, the rebel leader himself. Yigael Yadin, Masada's most famous excavator, connected the shards with Josephus's story of the last ten men drawing lots on the night before the Roman breach.

Of course Yadin and Josephus have their detractors. Especially among those opposed to the Zionist movement. Still, the fact remains, Masada has become the great and best symbol of independent Jewish nationalism and determination.

I have the script to prove it.

But back to Masada. . . . Down the road a ways from the mountain is the resort area of Ein Bokek. A modern, happening, flashy place. Lots of shopping and very nice, very *tall* hotels. You can slather yourself with mud, bob in the Dead Sea—you have to do it—and marvel at how that three-hundred-pound European guy wedged himself into that speedo, and then eat a cheeseless Big Mac at McDonald's. I like to go there sometimes. Most tour groups stay there.

But if you're on your own, check out Masada Hostel at the base of Masada itself. You almost don't notice the place. It rambles along, built into the foot of the mountain, the same color as the desert. Checking in can be a bit of a challenge if you don't speak Hebrew, but I've always found the staff very nice.

Except for the Two-Meat Guy.

The Two-Meat Guy is kind of a legend on our trips. He's been at the Masada each time I've stayed. You'll only find him behind the serving table in the dining hall. Can't miss him. Wearing a tall chef's hat, arms crossed, king of all he surveys. If someone—*anyone!*—takes more than two small pieces of meat, either on purpose or through simple ignorance, Two-Meat Guy points his ever-present tongs at the perpetrator and shouts, "Two meat!" Two-Meat Guy knows how to say at least this in both English and Hebrew. If the guilty three-meater doesn't return the stolen goods posthaste, Two-Meat Guy takes it upon himself to snatch the chicken leg, slice of beef, schnitzel, or whatever off the plate with his long tongs and return it to the chafing dish. Then he waves the embarrassed party on without another look.

I tried to make small talk with Two-Meat Guy once. Don't do that.

Also, never look Two-Meat Guy directly in the eye.

And, in the name of all that's holy, *always* only take two pieces of meat.

I checked into the Masada Hostel with Big Jim's group. The rooms weren't quite ready, so we left our bags in the tiled lobby and walked out onto the patio. I love the patio at the Masada Hostel. You can look east across the desert with its deep ravines, across the Dead Sea, all the way to the mountains in Jordan.

It's bare . . . broken . . . beautiful.

Jim's daughter, Meredith, asked me if we could hike the mountain the next morning rather than take the tram to the top. Now, I've heard that in speech classes, if someone asks you a question you're not quite sure about, they teach you to say, "I don't know the answer to that. Let me do some research, and I'll get back to you."

I never took speech class.

"Sure. Why not?" I said.

A few of the others wanted to do it as well. I'd never hiked the Snake Trail before, but I'd heard a little about it. I went in to the desk and began the linguistic gymnastics necessary to figure out the process. In the end it was simple. Make sure you have plenty of water, meet at the kiosk at the bottom of the mountain an hour and a half before sunrise, purchase a ticket or show the man your park pass, and off you go. Three or four of us agreed to meet in the lobby early the next morning.

True to the Masada Hostel desk-girl's word, there was indeed a man—half asleep—in the kiosk where she told me he would be. A dim bulb shone in the shack. I told him we were there to hike and showed him our passes.

"The trail is not open yet," he snapped. I wondered if he was related to Two-Meat Guy.

I looked around. Middle of the desert, nobody around, a ninety-minute hike ahead. I thought it was odd we couldn't just start. I looked at my watch. Technically he was right. Still three or four minutes till the time the girl had told me. With nothing else to do, Sleepy Kiosk Man and I stared at each other for most of the three minutes. Finally, he looked at his watch and said, "Okay, open."

That was it. Off we went.

The first thing I noticed was the dark. I'd figured—incorrectly—the entry to the path would be marked or lit somehow. After all, this was a major hiking destination, not the back edge of the South Dakota Badlands. Nope. *Figuring* doesn't always work in Israel. No light at all. We stumbled along for a bit, occasionally bumping into one another. I asked if anyone had a flashlight. Nope. Someone lit up their cell phone, and it helped a little.

I saw what I thought was a path or a rough road angling to the left. Must be it. I led out with only slightly more confidence than I felt. I stepped carefully, trying hard to make out every detail of the trail in the dim cell-phone light. Not so much for footing. More owing to the fact I don't like snakes. I knew the *Snake* Trail was named for its narrow, winding path up the cliff, but when I say *don't like,* I really mean *hate.* I can't stand the evil little suckers. This looked like snake country to me, and I could picture a thousand of them slithering in for the kill.

The path—definitely a path now—angled upward. A good sign since there was no doubt up was the right direction. Even better, my eyes were getting accustomed to the dark.

We walked on.

Then a little farther.

The path opened up into a gravel parking lot in front of a machinery storage shed.

"Hey, Buck, I don't think this is it," Meredith said.

"You might be right." I said, wishing in my loving, Christian heart that Two-Meat Guy was there to whack her with his tongs.

I heard voices off to the right. We walked over. Down a steep hill—a *very* steep hill—a group of hikers laughed and talked as they moved along a trail in the valley below. You know what they had?

Flashlights.

"We'll have to go back down the way we came and find the real trail," I said.

"We could just slide down the hill," somebody suggested.

Yeah, down a pitch-black, bottomless slope riddled with snakes in the middle of the desert is what I thought. "Okay, let's do it" is what I said.

Brilliant! We sat down and started sliding. It was a long, dusty slide. A million snakes watched our progress with beady little eyes. But somehow we all got to the bottom in one piece. We could see the other hikers off in the distance. All we had to do was follow.

The Snake Trail is steep and rocky and *hot*. A couple times I questioned myself as to the wisdom of the decision. Looking back I saw more hikers coming up the hill. As we wound back and forth, the sky over the Jordanian mountains lightened, the sun behind them in its dressing room getting ready for its grand entrance. The last bit of the hike was a series of metal stairs and catwalks. I was drenched by the time I stepped onto the plateau at the top. My CamelBak was sucked dry, but there was a place to refill. Good. I needed it.

My fellow travelers drifted off on their own, waiting for the sun. I climbed up on the thick wall edging the plateau and looked down. Far below I could make out the outline of General Silva's Roman encampments, still down there after two thousand years. I pictured Peter O'Toole looking up, giving me the King Arthur evil eye. What must that have been like? Marooned up there for three years, that small group of proud rebels watching, day after day, as the Roman war machine closed in?

A group of young IDF soldiers climbed up on the wall a few feet down from me. One held an Israeli flag high on a pole.

The sun cracked the sky over the mountains, sending bright sparkles across the Dead Sea.

The soldiers started to sing. Proud. Loud. I wanted badly to know the words.

An updraft caught the flag, and it spread, bright blue and white in the born-again light.

I listened to the soldiers and watched the sun inch up over the water. When it was well clear of the mountains, I climbed down and wandered a bit. Not far. I'd been here before a few times and didn't feel the urge to sightsee.

Israel is not a popular idea on the world stage. It's a *cup of trembling* in our day, just like Isaiah 51:22 said it would be.

Israel's enemies go by different names today, but Romans still build their camps around this hated people. The earthen ramp gets higher every year. And yet, there it is—this little country—existing, even thriving, against all odds, the blue flag with the white Star of David flying above it, riding the breeze against a morning sun. Yes, a testament to Eleazar and those who came after, but, even more, a monument to a living and faithful God.

There are those who claim that one day soon not a single inch of Israeli soil will exist—and they boldly add that then not one Jew will walk the earth ever again.

They shake their fists at heaven.

They scheme and plan and rattle their swords.

The sun rises on Masada.

God laughs.

That was my first hike up the Snake Trail, but not my last. And should God invite me back to that place, I'll do it again, as often as possible. I'll take a flashlight. I'll watch the sun rise and throw its rays on the sea. I'll look out over that beautiful, broken land.

And I'll listen to its song.

CHAPTER 22

Salad for Breakfast

"I said to myself: redemption will come only if their guide tells them,
'You see that arch from the Roman period?
It's not important: but next to it,
left and down a bit, there sits a man who's bought fruit
and vegetables for his family.'"

YEHUDA AMICHAI (EXCERPT FROM "TOURISTS")

The first time Michelle and I toured Israel, we loved our guide, Ami. I stand by my opinion that Israeli tour guides are the best in the world. Ami's passion for his homeland was contagious. He was tough, serious, joyful—*alive*. He was *Israel*. He shared more than history with us. He shared life. From Jerusalem to the Galilee to a wooden schooner on the Red Sea. We missed him when we left. Never forgot him. I'm sure there are a million travelers with comparable Israel-guide experiences.

I saw Ami again a few years later in a dining hall at one of the big hotels in Tiberias. I approached him and reintroduced myself. He squinted up at me and did a passable job of pretending he remembered who I was. He was kind enough to ask me to sit. I did. We talked awhile. I like to think he was happy to see I'd come back to Israel. He was interested in the fact I wasn't traveling with one of the tour groups.

The breakfast crowd pressed around us. Must have been at least two hundred bodies—sunscreened up and pumped for the day—jockeying for toast, cornflakes, and scrambled eggs.

Big tours, by simple mathematical necessity, use the big hotels. And the hotels do a great job providing meals. I find it fascinating to watch. Mainly because *American* and *kosher* are often a crazy-fun train wreck. Israeli hotels usually lay out a big spread for breakfast: salads, chopped cucumbers and tomatoes, hummus, pita, different types of cheese, yogurt, tuna . . . but please don't ask for a ham steak.

A woman dropped into a nearby chair. "Hey, Ami, you've got eggs in Israel. Why isn't there any bacon?"

Ami's face was priceless. "Is that a real question?"

"And why salad? Who eats salad for breakfast?"

"Israelis do. It's healthy."

"But no ranch dressing?"

"What's ranch dressing?" Ami said.

"Ranch *salad* dressing. You have all this lettuce and cucumbers and tomatoes but no ranch dressing. Or blue cheese. Or Thousand Island. Or French. It doesn't make sense."

Ami looked at me and shrugged.

I glanced at the woman's tray—a couple poached eggs, olives, cucumbers, lettuce—typical breakfast in Israel except for the big bowl of cornflakes next to her plate. I think the cornflakes were the hotel's nod to the red, white, and blue.

Hey, I can't point fingers. Back home I like the diner down the street for breakfast. Ham, eggs, biscuits and gravy—bring it on. I have a South African friend who shakes his head at the biscuits and gravy. He doesn't get it at all.

In Israel, back in the pioneer-kibbutz days, workers gathered early and ate whatever fresh produce was on hand. This healthy practice rolled over to following generations. No Pop-Tarts or Cap'n Crunch.

The woman poked at a piece of cucumber, sniffed it, discarded it, and then stuck a spoonful of cornflakes in her mouth.

I thought back to my very first trip to Israel with Ami. Another dining hall in a different hotel. Probably much the same cast of characters from his point of view—the world goes 'round. I remembered how much I'd enjoyed a tender piece of beef until I noticed it had taste buds of its own. That's when I learned Israelis like tongue. I finished it but without the same enthusiasm I'd started with. Just as good, but I couldn't shake the feeling of being tasted back.

Another memory from that night stood out. As I contemplated the unpleasantness of tongue, a woman from our group rushed up to the table, wide-eyed and breathless.

"I just saw (fill in the name of a famous American pastor or evangelist here). Come look! He just walked in! We need a picture!" She practically tripped over herself wriggling back through the crowd. Necks craned. People shifted and pressed in the direction of the famous arrival. I remember Ami popping an olive in his mouth, completely ignoring the commotion. He didn't have the least bit of interest in American celebrity culture.

I wondered if he remembered that night. I doubted it. He was probably used to our American idiosyncrasies. Not his first rodeo. But, still, what did a man like Ami think of us? I'd heard his story. He had fought in wars for the simple right to exist. Watched friends and brothers die in battle. And then dedicated his life to introducing foreigners to his love: the miracle called Israel, a desert garden clinging to the globe by the grace of God and the tenacity of its people. How many of Ami's relatives died in the Nazi gas chambers? How many from terrorist bombs? How many while battling for home and country? And here Ami was, defending salad and getting ready to load his millionth bus with sun hats and L.L.Bean safari vests.

And for some reason he looked happy about it.

"Ami, I think you're a patient guy," I said.

He shrugged. "*L'chaim!* Life is good."

That made me happy. Because life *is* good.

Still, for some reason I felt the need to apologize for the cornflake woman's insensitivity. All I could think of was "Hey, man, I don't need any bacon."

Ami grunted a laugh. "Or ranch dressing?"

I wanted to tell him I'd put him in a song—he was the soldier in "The Garden"—because his life and story had moved me.

I have listened to a soldier's pain
Of fallen friends and forgotten wars
As he spoke the sky began to rain
I watched the crowd as they turned to go
In the garden
The air is filled with minarets and mission bells
And all the things an aging soldier never tells

But I didn't tell him. Words felt too small an offering. I just shook his hand, said goodbye, and slipped back into the crowd with the rest of the revolving faces.

I've seen Ami a handful of times since. I always say hello. He always pretends to remember me.

L'chaim.

Life is good.

CHAPTER 23

Horse Trading

Esther Weiss's bantamweight Judaica store occupied the same corner in the Jewish Quarter of Jerusalem for years. We always looked forward to stopping there. Michelle made it her custom to buy a hat, but most of all we enjoyed chatting with Esther. An interesting lady with a serious horse trader's dickering skill. A lot like Michelle, actually. Good entertainment: the unstoppable force meets the immovable object.

We talked up Esther and her store to the group as we walked through the Armenian Quarter and past the bullet-pocked Zion Gate. But when we crossed into the Jewish Quarter, I was disappointed to find Esther and her shop gone, an Out of Business sign in the window.

We were about to move on when I saw, well above eye level, a piece of paper taped to the wall: *Esther Weiss* and an arrow pointing up a narrow street. Curious, I told the group to hold tight for a minute, and I walked in the direction of the arrow. I hadn't gone fifty steps when a tall, thin whirlwind of beard, ear curls, and flapping black clothes came barreling around a corner and almost crashed into me. The poor guy jerked back like I'd slapped him.

He lifted a long finger. "You can't be here! This area is off-limits to you."

No mystery. In his eyes, I was worldly and unclean. A mildly offensive perspective I usually try to let roll off my back when I encounter the Haredim.

I shrugged. "I'm only looking for Esther Weiss."

He narrowed an eye. "You know Esther Weiss?"

He pronounced it Esther *Veiss.*

"A little. I like to stop at her store and talk with her whenever I'm in Jerusalem. There was a sign—"

"What is your name?"

I told him, thinking *Buck Storm* had to be the most Gentile name on the planet—although, come to think of it, I'd known a Bucky Weinstein once. I could see his wheels turning.

"Wait here," he said.

I gave a thumbs-up.

"Right here! Don't move!" he said.

"I'm planted, *amigo.* Not going anywhere."

He headed back the way he'd come. A narrow lane led up a long stairway of Jerusalem stone. At the top, he ducked through a door-way on the right. Muted voices rolled down. At length he exited and came rolling back down the stairs, still not happy but maybe not quite as offended as before.

He pointed up. "It's there. Esther says you can come. But I tell you, go straight to her door and nowhere else. No farther and no other areas." He blew on by without waiting for a response, sideburn curls bouncing on the breeze.

I retrieved my group, and we headed up the stairs. From farther up the path, a couple Haredim men visually tracked our every move.

The doorway led to a small patio crowded with flowerpots and piles of boards. I knocked. The door swung, and Esther gazed out at me.

"Hi, Esther. I'm not sure if you remember me—"

"Of course! Come in!" She waved a hand at the piles of wood. "Watch your step. It's a booth leftover from *Sukkot*—the Feast of Tabernacles. I'm sorry. My apartment is very small."

I honestly don't know if Esther really remembered me or not. She must have met a million travelers over the years. I might have been nothing more than an opportunity to move some merchandise. Either way, even though there were several in our group, Esther warmly welcomed us into her home. I'll admit I was somewhat surprised. Invitation into a Jewish home isn't an everyday experience for foreign visitors.

Her place was tiny by American standards, though I knew the Jerusalem price tag must have been hefty. Stacks of merchandise from her store made the space even smaller. It looked like it had been a hasty exit.

"What happened to the store, Esther?" I said.

She shook her head. "Things change. What can I say? Several of us had to move. Can you imagine? We came here more than forty years ago—one of the first five original families to come after the Six-Day War. My daughter was the first baby girl born in the renewed Jewish Quarter." She smiled. "And now my store is going on the computer. I'm on-the-line."

"So no more physical location?"

She shrugged. "We'll see. It's Jerusalem, so you never know. Men plan; God laughs."

We talked for quite a while. The group was full of questions about life in the Old City. After a while, I asked her if she was still selling, letting her know we'd love to look at her wares. Esther the host smiled; Esther the horse trader smiled bigger.

Ladies and gentlemen, let the bargaining begin!

While Esther showed her merchandise, I let my eyes wander over a tall bookshelf stuffed with volumes, many religious. I'd asked Esther before on a previous trip if she was a believer in Yeshua, but she'd been noncommittal.

Shopping complete, someone suggested we pray before we left. Esther seemed happy to join in. I was glad. I would have loved to sit with her and talk longer, deeper, one-on-one, but I knew we'd stayed long enough. We thanked Esther and assured her we'd visit again.

As we left Esther's neighborhood, a couple kids played on the unforgiving stone street like it was park grass. Another bearded Orthodox passed us, eyes glued to his cell phone. It had been a great snapshot of Jerusalem life for us.

We spent the rest of the afternoon in the Old City. Western Wall, Burnt House Museum, a little time walking and shopping along the Cardo . . . a good day. We headed back to our rooms by the Jaffa Gate, had a cup of coffee, and rested awhile.

Later, showered and refreshed, we realized the evening lay before us. A beautiful, warm Jerusalem evening. As we gathered on the sidewalk, the city rattled and sang. Our group was ready to explore some more, and I knew just the place.

The sun hung low on the skyline, turning Suleiman's stonework to gold and sharp-edged shadows. One by one, lights flickered on as we exited the Jaffa Gate. A busker danced to a jangly tune on top of a wall by the stairs leading down to the Mamilla Mall. A serious character in top hat, tails, and striped tights. His accordion blew streamers of klezmer music out to the emerging stars.

Michelle held my hand.

I felt good.

We followed the outside of the wall awhile, then crossed over to Yafo Street and to the Light Rail stop. I waited in line at the automatic ticket machine. I had my shekels ready. Purchasing train passes is a process, and experienced guidance is a good idea your first time or two. First step—don't ask me why, it just *is*—rub your shekel vigorously next to the coin slot. You can tell the right spot to do this because the paint is worn off the machine from the million and two previous shekel-rubbers. Second step, drop in the freshly rubbed shekel. Third step, retrieve your unaccepted shekel from the change dispenser. Next, repeat these steps until the shekel is either accepted or the people in line behind you complain so loudly you get frustrated and pull out a credit card to pay with instead.

I made it three times through the steps before the credit card came out. It's a mystery to me how the Israelis can make improvements to an American fighter jet but can't seem to get simple ticket machines to work. I suppose it's all about priorities.

My group squeezed onto the train. Shoulder to shoulder in the car were stern, black-hatted Haredim, homemakers with babies in strollers, office workers in business suits, a couple of dreadlocked college students working on their laptops. If you want a taste of local everyday Jerusalem life, spend a little time on the Light Rail.

The group had scattered throughout the train car, finding any available space they could. I told the closest to me the name of the stop where we needed to get off and asked him to pass along the message. I prayed it would get through the car intact. When the Light Rail is busy, getting off against the crush of bodies getting on can be a challenge.

Jerusalem rushed by, and we clung to whatever we could reach to keep our balance. A few stops later the car only seemed to get more crowded. When our exit came, we wormed and squirmed. Out on the sidewalk I took a head count and was happy to see all present and accounted for.

I pointed behind me. "Welcome to The Shuk."

In the world's mind, as far as Israel goes, the Old City of Jerusalem is the star, front and center. It's the religious hub of the country. You might even say of the planet. The Old City is the stuff you see on the postcards. But if you really want to feel the heartbeat of Jerusalem, Machane Yehuda Market—or simply "The Shuk"— is the place to go. One time I heard an Israeli comedian describe the place as "Jewish Walmart on crack." That makes me laugh. I think the guy nailed it.

The Shuk is a mostly open-air market spread over a few blocks of downtown Jerusalem. The place is nonstop loud. Over two hundred and fifty vendors hawk everything you can imagine—and I mean *everything*. This is not a gift shop. Not an overpriced souvenir joint. It's a melting pot of young, old, wealthy, poor, religious, secular, and everyone in between. A hundred different walks of life collide at The Shuk in a menagerie of sight, sound, and smell. I love it, this E-ticket ride.

I told our band of gypsies to go forth and multiply. I gave three instructions: don't get lost (it would be hard to), meet back in three hours, and try some kind of food you've never had before.

Off they went.

The Shuk has hardware, clothes, electronics, pottery, fish, bread—if it's sellable, someone is selling it. But that night Michelle was on a mission. She was after *halva,* an interesting little piece of Middle Eastern heaven basically made from ground sesame butter and honey. I was game, so we started in.

As we walked, I watched a butcher—with a cigarette superglued to his bottom lip—hanging out over his counter and haggling full volume with an old woman in a head scarf. She shouted back in the Israel dickering language of Hebrew-and-hands. A lot of prices are marked, but at The Shuk, bargaining is elevated to a vociferous art form. At length the man gave a loud groan and exaggerated eye roll, tossed his cig, spat, and began wrapping a piece of meat. Clearly feeling like the victor, the woman crossed her arms and watched his work with a critical eye.

It didn't take long to find a place that sold halva.

"*Shalom,*" the young man said as we entered.

"*Shalom.* Do you speak English?" Michelle said.

"English, yes!"

"We'd like to buy some halva."

"Halva! Yes! Come, try. . . ."

They sold lots of flavors. We sampled.

Michelle pointed. "This one. But I only want a little slice."

"Yes. Just a slice," the guy repeated.

Just a slice turned into a pound. A pound sold for twenty-five bucks US.

"No, no. Just a slice," Michelle repeated.

The guy nodded and smiled, English suddenly forgotten.

They went at it for a while. A few prices were thrown around. A few minutes later we left with a pound for around fifteen bucks. Everybody looked happy.

Cheese, nuts, fish, fruit, candy, bread. . . . We moved through the market. I stopped short at a bakery. Exactly what I'd been waiting for: an acre of chocolate butter croissants. Traveler's tip: if you've never had an Israeli chocolate butter croissant, set down this book, get on a plane, and get yourself to The Shuk. I'm telling you, those little beauties are like biting into a baby angel.

I fished a few shekels out of my pocket.

"Wait, wait!" The shopkeeper held up a hand and disappeared into the back. He came back twenty seconds later with another tray, this one straight from the oven.

"Can I live at your house?" I said.

"My house is small. I'll sell you a croissant instead."

"Sell me five."

"Even better."

I had something I'd run across on a previous trip I wanted to show Michelle.

"Follow me. I gotta show you something," I said to her.

"If you keep eating those croissants, you won't be hard to spot."

Wives are good like that.

We exited the market onto Agripas Street and turned right. I stopped after a hundred feet or so and pointed. "Here it is."

"Here what is?"

"Read the sign."

"Best Falafel in Israel."

"See?"

"You think this is the best falafel in Israel?"

"Signs don't lie."

"Signs lie all the time."

A guy leaned behind the counter, his forearms thick and hairy. I asked him, "Hey, is this really the best falafel in Israel?"

He grabbed some tongs, dropped a falafel ball on a napkin, and handed it to us.

We split it. I could probably live on falafel and chocolate croissants.

And maybe tacos.

We ordered to go and ate as we walked, everything around us loud and warm.

We met the others back at the Light Rail stop. Everyone was laden with bags and stories. An Orthodox man dozed in his seat as we boarded the train. A few teenagers laughed in the back. Otherwise the train was empty, a different world than when we'd come. Outside the Jaffa Gate, the busker had packed his accordion and top hat and retired for the night. The city lay quiet, resting up for another blue-sky day.

Later, Michelle and I lay in bed listening to ancient stone breathe and settle. I thought about Esther and her husband, their grown children—all of them so precious to God—and the family's long history in the Old City. Their lives, a link in a historical chain reaching back all the way to Melchizedek's Salem. Esther was very good at talking with Christians. What did she think of Jesus? Was she intrigued? Drawn? Or did she wonder, like so many Jews, *If He was the Messiah, why did He leave us in such a mess?* I hoped our visit had been a good witness.

"That was nice of Esther to ask us in today," I said.

Michelle softly spoke her tired agreement.

"I wonder if she's a believer? Sometimes—with some of the

things she says—I think she might be. And she prayed with us before we left."

"I wonder too."

Moonlight shone through a high-up window. A dog barked.

I listened to my wife breathe in the darkness. "It *was* good falafel," I said after a while.

But she was already asleep.

CHAPTER 24

Going Down

"That's not rust. It's blood that has never dried."

YEHUDA AMICHAI

The Old City of Jerusalem is built, layer upon layer, on the triumphs and car crashes of those who've gone before. It's a tall pile of stones and bones supporting a living, breathing *now*. History discovered, reconstructed, imagined, and repeated, four thousand years in the making, one generation building upon the successes and failures and destruction of the previous.

In contrast, they say, Americans live in a microwave culture: we expect everything fast. I don't think so. I think we left our microwaves back in the nineties with desktop computers and dial-up internet. We've moved past *fast* and straight to *instantaneous*. No more waiting for the tubes to warm up, man. Give it to me *yesterday*—food, church, work, sports, and especially relationships.

Oh, Israelis are wired for speed, no doubt. You can even get a good cell signal in the middle of the Negev. (Once a friend called me in the States from a Bedouin tent!) But as far as relationships go—even basic conversations—Israel is not America. A fact that often equates to disappointment morphing into frustration when a tourist hops off the bus with a supersecret pocketful of Gospel tracts (printed in Hebrew—planned ahead) and a plan to save God's chosen peeps in a single, sunny afternoon. A few hours later the same pilgrim climbs back onboard, unsuccessful and disgruntled (unless they got to snap a pic of themselves saving the grifter on the steps in the Jewish Quarter) and wondering why the Jews are so stinkin' unfriendly. Well, truth is, they're *not* unfriendly. They just don't know you.

In Israel, like the Arab culture, relationships are a long-haul, slow-burn proposition. They start over coffee. Always coffee. There are conversations, maybe superficial at first, but going ever deeper. There is growth. Eventually little cracks appear in our masks, and some real life seeps out. And then, one day—it may be years later—comes an invite to dinner. Coffee becomes a meal in someone's home. In their sanctuary. And a friendship starts.

By that time you can't even remember where you left all those Romans Road tracts.

I think of the city of Jerusalem in the same way. It's an elusive friendship that takes time to develop. A cursory tour—the Wall, the Temple Mount, the museums—are like a first cup of coffee. We're moved, we're enamored, we're spiritually stimulated, but we're certainly not invited to dinner.

Because beneath the worn stones of the tourist paths, beneath the markets and shops, synagogues and cathedrals, there are more stones. And beneath those, even more.

The city is deep, complicated, secretive.

Jews see Jerusalem through their religious and sociopolitical lenses. How could they not? Jewish archaeologists dig for *Jewish* things. It's a good thing to seek out and bolster the history of your people. Palestinians usually focus on the Muslim angle when looking at the city's history. Both angles are valid because both sides of history happened.

Take the long walk back to Genesis 14. There you'll find the first mention of Jerusalem, when Melchizedek, king of Salem, is referenced. That was during Abraham's lifetime, over four thousand years ago. Historians tell us Jerusalem is one of the oldest cities in the world. Attacked over fifty times that we know about; captured and recaptured forty-four times; besieged twenty-three; and completely wiped out twice. Canaanite, Judah, Greek, Roman, Byzantine, the Caliphates, Crusader, Ottoman . . . the list goes on. Layer after layer of movements, ideologies, and civilizations destroying and rebuilding on the shoulders of old ghosts.

From the Galilee, I emailed my friend Ronny Simon, who is an author, Israel scholar, and one of the country's very best tour guides. I told him I was on my way with several of my friends and family. There'd been some violence in the news—a slew of terrorist-instigated stabbings—and I wanted to know what was safe and what wasn't. Usually what we hear on Western news is hyped and exaggerated. I expected that to be the case. But Ronny answered with a different tone: "Don't go into any Muslim neighborhoods. Avoid the Damascus Gate. Avoid the Garden Tomb. Don't go out at night. . . ." He went on.

"What about the Western Wall Tunnels?" I wrote.

"I wouldn't. Not with a group. I doubt they will even let you in."

A big disappointment for me. Especially since I had my family traveling with me. I think of the tunnels as kind of a hot cup of joe with the grand lady herself. A way to step back in time. But things were tense, and the exit happens to pop up right smack in the Muslim Quarter.

The portion of the Western Wall most people experience when visiting or see in pictures and on TV, is exactly sixty-two feet long. It wasn't originally built for prayer. Or for tourists. Or to stick little paper prayers in. It was built as a retaining wall, constructed as part of the expansion of the Second Jewish Temple by Herod the Great, a couple decades before Jesus came on the scene. Sixty-two feet of the wall sees sunlight and feels praying hands, but duck underground and you'll find that the entire structure stretches over *sixteen hundred feet.*

In the mid-nineteenth century, British archaeologist Charles Wilson began excavating the wall. He was followed shortly by his bookend, Charles Warren. Both made significant historical finds, digging deep under the city and uncovering large portions of the wall going back to the Second Temple period and Herod the Great's reconstruction.

From 1948 to 1967 Eastern Jerusalem was under Jordanian control. This meant Jews had no access to their holiest sites, including the Western Wall of the Temple Mount. They couldn't pray there, let alone dig.

Then came the Six-Day War.

You see, Israel as a new nation was a big, throbbing thorn in the paw of the Muslim world. In June of 1967 Egypt mobilized troops along its border with Israel. Not good. The Israelis smelled trouble. Launching preemptive airstrikes and ground offensives, they took the Sinai Peninsula by force and surprise. Syria to the north and Jordan to the east jumped into the fight. Overwhelming odds. Things looked bleak for the Jews. But think what you will about Israel, the IDF is arguably the best fighting force on the planet. Not only did they win the day, but they took back control of East Jerusalem, the West Bank, and the Golan Heights. Fewer than a thousand Israelis were killed. The Arabs lost more than twenty times that. There's a saying in Israel today: "Please attack us. We need more land."

Thus, the reunification of Jerusalem. And access to pray at the Western Wall once again. Emotional tears were shed by bloody and battle-hardened soldiers at the first glimpse of those holy stones.

Free to excavate again, the Ministry of Religious Affairs of Israel picked up the baton. They dug and explored for twenty years. Beneath their shovels the Old City offered up new secrets.

And I really wanted to show them to my family and friends.

So while they took some time at the Western Wall, I headed for the back of the plaza and the unremarkable tunnel entrance. A young man stood there as I approached. I told him I'd made an appointment online months before and asked if there was any way we'd still be able to go in.

"Absolutely."

After my correspondence with Ronny, I was surprised. "What about the exit into the Muslim Quarter? I don't want to take a group out there right now," I said.

He told me the exit was closed—barred and padlocked—but we could retrace our route back through the tunnel and exit where we entered.

Nice. We were back on.

I rounded up my group, and at our appointed time, we climbed down some stairs and stepped back in history two thousand years. The noise of the square above hushed. The air became close and holy. Down more stairs and through large, caverned rooms to the underground portion of Herod's massive retaining wall. We took our time, running our hands along the Western Stone, one of the heaviest objects ever lifted by humans without the aid of modern machinery. I'd seen the Western Stone a few times, but it still rocked me back on my heels. A monolith, nearly forty-five feet long and ten feet high, solid stone practically the size of a semitrailer. The edges of all Herod's stones were beautifully beveled and carved so perfectly a piece of paper couldn't fit between them.

Farther on we came to a small room. Several women sat praying, voices low and deep with emotion. This point of the wall is considered the closest Jews can get to their holiest place, the spot where the Holy of Holies once housed the Ark of the Covenant, now home to the Al Aqsa Mosque and Dome of the Rock. To continue on, we needed to pass through the praying women.

As many times as I've been through the Rabbinical Tunnels, moving through this group of intercessors always gives me pause. It's an intrusiveness I find incredibly awkward. In fact, when I think of all the places in Israel I've visited, it's this tiny area deep under the city where I feel most like a foreigner. Most people are respectful, but I've seen some groups walk through the spot talking loudly, laughing, even snapping pictures. Humanity at its self-centered, calloused best.

I explained this to my group, and we walked through the space quickly and quietly. I was glad when the women continued their petition and took no notice of our passing.

A bit farther on, the walkway beneath our feet turned to clear plexiglass. Excavations through the centuries plunged to incredible depths. I imagined King Solomon, King David, the judges—history so varied, so complex, could anyone ever really know it? Where, in those stony depths, were the paths of the prophets? The blood of

Stephen? The bones of Nicodemus? No doubt, Jerusalem is a secret keeper. Sharing some, but holding more. The vast majority of the short, earthly stretches of its inhabitants are nothing but whispers. Smoke on the wind.

We ended our hike along an ancient Hasmonean water tunnel and an underground pool. Sure enough, the exit was barred and padlocked. We retraced our steps the way we'd come in, enjoying the experience just as much on this second pass.

Sixteen hundred feet later, we climbed back to the twenty-first century, a tired handful of Rip Van Winkles. Night had found the city during our time underground. We walked back past the Wailing Wall with its faithful few and then up the street. We passed a café. A group of teens sat around a table, laughing. Music played. A shofar blew somewhere. A couple walked by, a little boy on a tricycle next to them. The woman's head was covered by a scarf. The man had a pistol tucked in the back of his pants. They didn't look our way. They didn't ask us to coffee.

But that's okay.

Because Jerusalem, like the people who live there, is a slow burn. But, thankfully, consider this one promise: one day, maybe soon, for those who look forward to Jesus's imminent return, the ultimate dinner invitation awaits.

CHAPTER 25

Two ...
or Maybe Three ...
Things

I've seen the boardwalk along the Sea of Galilee asleep at sunrise and busy in the afternoon loading tourist boats, but by night it's a different world. Kind of "county fair meets California's boisterous Venice Beach."

One night, Michelle and I paused to watch some young kids playing on an abandoned bungee ride. The giant slingshot kind you see at roadside carnivals. No barker, though. Nobody running the thing at all. Not an adult in sight. A few boys strapped another in, yanked him down, then launched him thirty feet in the air. He bounced around awhile before landing. One of his friends shoved him out of the way and climbed into the harness. Broken bones waiting to happen. I wondered where the nearest emergency room was, thinking at the same time about the guys I'd grown up with and how we'd have been doing the exact same thing.

I walked into a little store to get some ice cream for us. As I paid,

I heard yelling. I stepped out and saw Michelle working her way out from the fence around the bungie ride.

I ran over. A few of the boys were gone. The two still there didn't look happy. One held a hand to his bloody lip.

"What happened?" I said.

She pointed. "They were picking on that little guy. One of them was holding him, and the others started punching him. I made them stop."

"You went in there?"

"They were *punching* him!"

My wife the vigilante with Guy Clark's playground sense of justice. I love her. Don't mess with her.

We walked awhile. Michelle went into a shop. I waited on the sidewalk with my ice cream, people watching.

Then I saw him coming, his eyes fixed on me. The kind of moment when you know, even though there's a crowd around, someone has you and only you in his sights. A big man. Shirt untucked and unbuttoned halfway down his chest. Beard, dark and thick. His hair hadn't seen a comb in a while, and the yarmulke perched on the back of his head might have hidden a bald spot. I remember him clearly, even his worn sandals, thick feet, and toenails that needed a trim.

But what I remember most were the two fingers he held up as he walked toward me. Like an angry peace sign. An oxymoron if I'd ever seen one.

"Two!" he said when he got close enough. "Two things!"

I'm sure my confusion registered.

"You're from America, right?" he said.

I licked my newly purchased ice cream bar, fighting the age-old cold ice cream versus warm night battle. "Yes."

The fingers again. "Two things!"

"Okay. Two things. . . . What two things?"

"Two things you can't mention when you talk to me."

Didn't know the guy. Didn't know we were supposed to have a conversation. But I figured I was in it now, so I might as well play. "Okay. I'll bite. What two things?"

He dropped his fingers into a fist and then let his index flick back up. "One. Obama." The middle followed the index. "Two. Clinton."

I certainly had no skin in the game. "I can do that. No problem. Hillary or Bill?"

"Hillary or Bill what?"

"You said I can't mention Clinton. Hillary or Bill?"

"Both."

I tick my own fingers up, one, two, three. "Obama. Hillary. Bill. That's technically three things."

"I don't care. Don't mention them. You like Obama?"

"What about Chelsea?"

"What Chelsea?"

"Another Clinton."

"No Clintons. You like Obama?"

"See, Obama's the very first thing you said we're not supposed to mention, so you're already breaking your own rule." Pointing out the obvious is one of my gifts.

He shook his head. "The rules apply to you, not me. You're American, so you can't come here and talk about them, period."

"I wasn't planning on talking about them. I'm just eating ice cream and waiting for my wife. You're Israeli?"

"I am now. Since '85."

"Where were you before that?"

"New Jersey."

I introduced myself, and he did the same. Funny, I remember his feet and thick toenails but not his name. I wish I did.

He pointed. "Your ice cream's melting."

I licked again.

"You know what? We loved Obama here at first. His approval ratings were off the charts. But, in the long run, he's been very bad for Israel," he said.

"I can't argue with that."

"So you don't like him?"

"I don't like his politics so far, but I honestly always hope a president does well. It doesn't make sense to me when people root for a leader to fail just because he's from another party. It's bad for the country. Bad for everyone."

"Well, Hillary hates Israel."

"She says she doesn't."

"It's not about what she *says*. They all *say*. It's what she does that counts."

"True."

"When you're *here*, when they're doing it to *you*, you feel it, you know?"

I said I did. Then, "I think Hillary likes the Palestinian part of Israel."

He grunted and shrugged. "You've met Palestinians?"

"Of course. I think my wife even met a few Palestinians over by that bungee thing a few minutes ago."

"She should be careful."

"That's what I told her."

"Israeli Jews are nothing but political pawns to the West. Obama ran to the Middle East to make sure everyone was happy, but he skipped Israel. How do you think we felt about that?"

"I didn't like it either. A lot of Americans were embarrassed by how he handled that."

"That's good. You *should* be embarrassed. It was wrong. The US is supposed to be our ally, but we wonder if it's still the case."

I thought of something. "You remind me of a guy I once talked to in the Muslim Quarter. He was carrying a bucket of fish. He asked me if I was a Christian, so I told him yes. Then he got right in my face and said, 'Bill Clinton was the best president the United States ever had.'"

"He was definitely Palestinian. They loved Clinton."

"Uh-huh. I think he wanted to pick a fight."

"Maybe. Or maybe just push you a little."

"I asked him about Carter since Carter's so big on Palestine. He said, 'Yes, Carter was good too.' He talked for a while. He *definitely* liked Carter. Then I asked him what my being Christian had to do with Bill Clinton. He said no Christians voted for Clinton."

"That's true," the New Jersey Jew agreed.

"Not really," I replied. "I personally know some Christians who voted for him."

"Anyway, there's no such thing as Palestine. It's not a country. Show me Palestinian money? Borders? Language? There's *Israel*. We're all *Israelis*."

"Okay."

"That man was the only Palestinian you've met?"

"No. I've met lots of Palestinians. I feel bad for the Palestinian Christians. They're kind of a forgotten group, even by a lot of the American church. But the Muslim guy in the Old City is the only one I remember stopping me to talk specifically about politics like you did. Maybe you're related."

He shrugged. "At least by Abraham."

A nightclub thumped bass behind closed doors. A couple emerged, and music blasted the night for a few seconds, then back to just the thump as the door swung shut. Every shop and stand on the boardwalk was open and crowded. A riot of light and color and noise. In front of one shop, electric toy cars chased each other. Down the way a couple guys were setting up a sound system next to a wide promenade. On the Galilee, tour boats bobbed at anchor, tired from a long day of chugging over watery Messianic footprints. Out past the boats, only darkness.

My new friend—if I could call him that, jury was still out—looked thoughtful. Then he said, "One thing I don't understand about that Muslim in the Old City. . . ."

"Why he thought no Christians voted for Bill Clinton?"

"No, why he had a bucket of fish."

"At least I think it was fish. Maybe I remember it wrong."

"Does it matter?"

"I guess not."

"Then why did you mention it?"

"I have no idea," I said.

"Neither do I."

"Would you ever go back to New Jersey?" I asked him.

"Why would I? Israel is the greatest nation on earth. We are blessed by God."

"I like coming to Israel."

"Then you are blessed by God too."

"New Jersey isn't blessed by God?"

He smiled. "New Jersey is definitely not blessed by God."

"So, I have to say, you realize we've talked about all three things I wasn't supposed to mention, right?"

"Two things."

"Technically three."

He nodded. "Okay, three. Yes. This has been a horrible conversation." He shook my hand again. "I'm a Messianic Jew. I'm glad you know Yeshua. Thank you for coming to Israel. Now, go home and vote out Obama."

"Nice to meet you too. And I'll see what I can do."

"But let's not mention him."

"My lips are sealed."

He held his peace sign up over his head again as he walked off.

"Two things," I said.

"Two things," he called back.

CHAPTER 26

The Fountain of Tears

The sun was only an hour old, still working its slow grind up out of Jordan and over the Dead Sea. Alone on the Masada Hostel patio, I sipped coffee and watched its progress. No tree or canvas covering offered shade. Soon the heat would chase me inside. My little traveling band would go down to the Dead Sea and float later, but we had some extra time in the day.

I texted my friend Dan Stolebarger: *I'm down at Masada. Have some time. What about* The Fountain of Tears? *Can you give me contact info?*

For a long time I'd been curious about the sculpture called *The Fountain of Tears*. A visual dialogue of suffering between arguably the two most horrible events in human history, the latter especially so in the Jewish mind: the crucifixion of Jesus Christ and the Jewish Holocaust. I'd heard snatches about the sculpture here and there but hadn't yet had free time in the area to make the trek myself. I knew it was big, but that's about it. It definitely wasn't on the normal tourist route.

You have to see it for yourself, people would say.

And today I had some time. Today of all days: 27th of Nisan on the Jewish calendar. Yom HaShoah, Holocaust Remembrance Day in Israel.

I'm sure you can imagine, Holocaust Remembrance Day is observed with the utmost somber reverence and respect in Israel. Ceremonies and memorial services are held throughout the country. Quiet grieving is the order of the day. After all, there is no Jew who hasn't been affected by the Holocaust. Public places of entertainment are closed by law. At exactly 10:00 a.m., air raid sirens sound across the country, and everyone pauses for a mandatory two minutes of silent reflection. Motorists actually stop in the middle of the road, wherever they happen to be, get out, and stand by their cars. It's a powerful, moving sight. A nation, unified in loss, determined not to let history be repeated.

Yes, a good day for a handful of wandering Americans to visit *The Fountain of Tears*. Maybe even a good way to offer our respect.

My cell dinged. Dan, telling me the sculpture was in Arad, a desert town not far from us. He added a phone number. I called it. Dafna, the sculptor's wife, answered. A friendly woman. I explained who I was and that Dan had given me the contact info. She was familiar with Dan and said, "Sure, come on up." She told me her husband, Rick Wienecke, would probably be out, but someone would be there to show us around. She gave me directions, which I only half listened to, figuring our GPS would fill in the gaps. We agreed on an approximate time.

After breakfast my *compadres* and I hit the van, and I punched *Fountain of Tears* into the Elvis GPS. Of course Elvis couldn't find it. I tried a simple search for Arad instead. No problem there. The King gave us a *Thumbs-up, baby,* and we hit the road, winding the short drive down from Masada and picking up Highway 90 heading south. The Dead Sea shone on our left. On our right, heat waves danced out on the desert. Ein Bokek loomed in the distance, tempting us with its air-conditioned spaces and cold drinks. But we had a plan, Stan. We barreled right on past the high-rises and big, black Aroma coffee cup.

Near the tiny settlement of Neve Zohar, we turned west onto Highway 31 and began a slow climb up through the desert. Looping turns intermittently treated us to wide, CinemaScopic views, a panorama of wadis and flat-topped hills. Brown, barren, hot—the kind of country Louis L'Amour would say was "hell on horses and women." The sun directly above us now, it was a hundred degrees at least. I dropped the van into second gear, praying our radiator held.

We drove on.

In my head Arad was a small, out-of-the-way place. A few dusty, desert streets laid out in a grid. The kind of tiny burg that would make a semifamous, sixty-foot-long, twelve-foot-high sculpture easy to find. Of course, Arad was *not* what I had pictured in my head. I should have known better. Perched in the Kidod Range on the southwestern edge of the Judean Desert, the town turned out to be good-sized. Almost twenty-five thousand people. Quite a mix of cultures—Jews, Bedouins, Christians, Black Hebrews—called it home. It was cooler up there, and the streets were busy with life. I liked the place right off the bat. We'd climbed for over an hour from below sea level, leaving almost eighteen hundred feet and twenty degrees behind us.

A beautiful day in a beautiful place.

I also realized finding *The Fountain of Tears*—housed in a guy's backyard—might not be the simple prospect I'd imagined. Of course, as the fearless leader (this wingding had been my idea, after all),

I didn't necessarily want to announce to the group the possibility that Elvis and I might be a tad in the dark about the route to our destination. I tried again the number Dan had given me but got no answer this time.

Guess I should have listened better to Dafna.

I called an audible. "Hey, let's have lunch." When in doubt, find something to eat.

Cheerful agreement all around.

To tell you the truth, I wasn't all that worried. Things have a way of working out in Israel. And my cotravelers were easy. Actually, they'd probably kind of like the idea of being lost. And, besides, I was hungry.

We found a place to park next to a central plaza. Lots of stores, people wandering around, and some promising-looking hole-in-the-wall eateries. We strolled for a while, our mood light and casual. We wandered through a couple of stores. Eventually we found a little shawarma place. The owner only spoke Hebrew, but like good Americans, we made up for it by talking louder in English. In the end, the universal language of pointing and hand gesturing got us loaded down with sustenance and seated around a couple shaded plastic tables out on the sidewalk. Turned out to be one of the best restaurants I'd been to in Israel. Life was good.

At least it *would* be good if I could manage to find *The Fountain of Tears*—the whole reason we'd driven all that way in the first place.

Occasionally, a curious passerby would stop and chat, wondering what the Westerners were doing there. A man approached. Lanky, tan, and fit. He helped himself to a chair and leaned his elbows on the table. "Americans?"

"Uh-huh. Sounds like you are too."

He affirmed the fact. We talked awhile. It was clear after only a few minutes that we'd acquired a cheerful, self-appointed tour guide. Fine with me. My friends and I asked a lot of questions. He laid out Arad's demographic makeup and history. It really was a fascinating place. Originally planned as a tourist town serving the Dead Sea set, that idea floundered and sank when the big hotels went in at Ein Bokek, and Arad was relegated to backwater status. (Reminded me of the Old West American towns that got bypassed by the railroad.) The locals didn't count the lack of tourists a bad thing, though. Besides, in the end, the clear air and high-desert beauty attracted a different crew. From Orthodox to hippie New Agers and a whole slew of people in between.

We talked about Israel, the Holocaust, and what it meant to be a country feeling alone in an anti-Semitic, hostile world.

"So what brings you guys up?" he asked at length.

"We came to see *The Fountain of Tears* sculpture," I said. "Have you heard of it?" *Please say yes, man. . . .*

He grinned. "No joke? Yeah. I'm actually remodeling their bathroom. I'm headed over now. You want to follow me?"

I love God. I've come to understand—with a lot of miles under my wheels—when we finally come to the end of ourselves and lean back into our Father's arms, He delights in surprising us with little joys.

"That sounds perfect," Elvis and I said in unison.

Back to the van. As we zigzagged through the streets, I realized what a huge blessing God provided us in our newfound friend. The place definitely wasn't easy to find. Finally, on the outskirts of town, we pulled onto the gravel and dirt behind a large tent next to a house. Our friend waved us in and said he'd let someone know we were there.

It was cool and quiet inside. Water trickled. We took seats at the back of the tent opposite the sculpture. The piece, lit with soft light, was so wide it was impossible to get it all on the first look. Seven white Jerusalem stone panels separated by six stone pillars. I noticed water dripping down the pillars—the origin of the trickling sound. In each stone panel, a crucified Christ figure leaned out from His cross above a life-sized bronze depiction of a Holocaust victim. Seven images of crucifixion. Seven bone-thin victims of the Holocaust. The body language between the figures—physically depicting Jesus's crucifixion statements and the Holocaust victim's reactions to them—was so intense I struggled to take it in.

A man entered and greeted us. We introduced ourselves, and he began to explain what we were seeing.

Oh, that my head were waters,
And my eyes a fountain of tears,
That I might weep day and night
For the slain of the daughter of my people!
—Jeremiah 9:1

The six pillars of stone, he told us, represented the six million who lost their lives in the Jewish Holocaust, and the continual flow of water, God's tears. The Christ figure in each of the seven panels silently depicted one of the seven phrases Jesus uttered in His agony as, below, the Holocaust victims reacted to His words.

Good art will often offend. It will draw. It will move. A gamut of emotions hammered me as each minute, each panel, each bronze drew me deeper into the story.

I wanted to leave. I wanted to stay. I wanted to cry.

How, I wondered, *could the artist have gone there?* I knew the Jewish mind-set. I knew what I was seeing. Not a photo; not a drawing. Something permanent—carved from *Jerusalem* stone. Stone that Jesus Himself might have touched, might have walked on. What my eyes were seeing must be so incredibly hard—so offensive, even—to the Jewish people. Jesus Christ in the *Holocaust?* In the single historical event most Jews believe led to the attempted extermination of their entire race. Unprecedented in human history. But there He was, Jesus, the sin of the world pinning Him to a cross, looking down into the immense and unimaginable pain of the attempted Jewish extermination.

A dialogue of suffering.

I thought I might try to describe every panel in this account. Go through it scene by scene.

I won't.

Because I can't. I can't even begin to come close to doing Rick's work justice.

Even as I write, the emotion of that day comes back. Let me just say this: *The Fountain of Tears* humbled me, it tumbled me, and in the end it left me nowhere to go but to Christ.

Israel has been a land of miracles from the beginning. That day was full of them. The fact that our visit fell on Holocaust Remembrance Day. Running into our impromptu guide. And, most of all, the sculpture itself—a testament to the faithfulness of the artist and of gifts given to men. And, even more, a testimony to the faithfulness of God and His Son, crucified, buried, resurrected—offering healing to the nations.

We all were quiet as we drove out of Arad and down through the hills. Humbled. To this day, whenever I have the opportunity to talk with my fellow pilgrims from that trip, they say seeing *The Fountain of Tears* was the experience that most moved them.

Once, over dinner in Phoenix, Arizona, I asked my friend and veteran Israeli guide Ronny Simon what he thought of *The Fountain of Tears*.

He shook his head. "The artist combined what Jews consider the two most horrible things to ever happen to our race—the crucifixion of Jesus and the Holocaust."

Then he changed the subject.

I didn't press.

It was true. Many Jews believe the crucifixion of Jesus gave—and continues to give—many in the world an excuse for blatant and often violent anti-Semitism. And I can see how they would think it—their suffering has been immense.

Thomas Moore, the Irish poet, wrote, "Earth has no sorrow that Heaven cannot heal." And, oh, what sorrow! The Holocaust is a horrible blight on the human story. We should all feel deeply about it. I *do* feel deeply about it. *But,* I ask myself, *how can I really understand the pain and horror the way the Jews can?* So I pray deeply, and I have to trust that, one day, *all* of us—Jew and Gentile alike—will come face-to-face with the Only Reality. The relentless flood of *Him*.

I pray healing for my Jewish friends. Healing that can come only from God.

We look forward.

Dreaming and hoping and praying for that upside-down, backward holocaust of *Love* and *Light* and *Life* that will leave no survivors.

The Jews are a race that must be totally exterminated.

HANS FRANK
GOVERNOR GENERAL IN NAZI-OCCUPIED POLAND, 1944

Remember only that I was innocent and, just like you, mortal on that day. I, too, had a face marked by rage, by pity and by joy. Quite simply, a human face!

BENJAMIN FONDANE
MURDERED AT AUSCHWITZ, 1944

"Come to Me, all who are weary and heavy-laden, and I will give you rest."

JESUS CHRIST

CHAPTER 27

They Will Come

I had a conversation with a Saudi Arabian woman once. She told me when she was young, her father would tell her and her sisters bedtime stories. Sometimes for hours. A very unusual thing for a Saudi Muslim man to do. Before she left the country to go to college, he did another unusual thing. He encouraged her to seek out knowledge with an open mind. Even to observe the differences between the Jesus of Islam and the Jesus of Christianity. "Explore. Learn," he said.

And she took his advice. Not long after that conversation, she found herself in America. An opportunity arose: a group of people gathering to study the Christian Bible. She decided to honor her father and check it out.

Muslims recognize Jesus as one of the great prophets. In fact, a quick perusal of Islamic writings will quickly and clearly show you that much of the Q'ran was recycled from the Bible. "But," Islamic scholars will say, "the Q'ran doesn't *copy* the Bible; it *corrects* the Bible."

(Because God couldn't quite get it right the first time?)

Mary is the only woman mentioned by name in the Q'ran. It even references the virgin birth of Jesus. It describes Him as *good*. As a prophet and a man. In the Q'ran, however, Jesus had the *appearance* of being crucified but was rescued by Allah at the last minute. So, no death and *absolutely* no resurrection. This is why the inscription on the Dome of the Rock at the Temple Mount is essentially an entire sermonette denouncing the divinity of Jesus. It's long and involved, but boiled down to its essence, it essentially says *God has no son*.

So, it's interesting that when my Saudi friend braved the Christian gathering, they opened the Bible to the book of John, the Gospel that most fully illuminates Jesus as God and Savior. Then something strange. . . . As the group read and discussed, the stories about the Christian Jesus began to sound familiar. She'd heard them somewhere before.

Her father's bedtime stories.

All those years he'd been communicating the Jesus of the Bible to her. He'd used a different name but, no doubt, the same stories. She wanted to dig deeper. To understand this concept of God as Love, not fear. She began to compare and weigh the God of Christianity with the God of Islam.

And, as true seekers inevitably will be, she was wrecked by His grace. She discovered in the Bible a God who loved her and desired her. A God who would give His only Son for her rescue.

A God who said, *"Now that you know, daughter—now that you've heard—what will you do in response to My Son?"*

She took the hand of Jesus.

We talked long, she and I. What a beautiful story.

"But," she said at length, "may I ask you a question?"

"Of course," I said.

"The God of the Bible is so great. So wonderful. Why are Christians so weak?"

"What do you mean?"

"In America, for example. God has rescued them. Given them so much. But they are happy to live in their sin. They say, 'Grace! Grace!' and continue to live any way they like. Even some of the pastors! And they're supposed to be men of God?"

I had to admit, she had a point. "All I can say is look to Jesus. All men, no matter how good or well-intentioned, will let you down."

"You included?"

"*Definitely* me included."

She went on. "And it is not only in America. God is so strong! But when Muhammad first began his spread of Islam, the Christians rolled over without a word! Why? And, last, what about Israel? I don't understand. In the very land where Jesus was crucified and resurrected, there are practically no Christians. Where are the Christians?"

A great question.

One with a lot of answers—the brutal march of history, an adversary doing his best to destroy and kill, the basic selfishness of man. . . . What could I tell her?

Where *are* the Christians in Israel? . . .

First, let me give you a quick tour of Jerusalem. There are technically nine gates in the walls of Jerusalem's Old City. Eight are passable. All are worth a visit if you have the time. From the Mount of Olives, you look down on the Eastern or Golden Gate beneath the Temple Mount. As I mentioned earlier, due to Jewish claims that the Messiah will one day use the Golden Gate to access the Temple, it's been sealed and unsealed a few times through the ages, and today it's walled in with stone. A job accomplished in 1541, during the Ottoman Empire, by Suleiman the Magnificent. You can Google *Suleiman*. He was quite a character. Look for the guy with a pointy beard and a huge, bubble-shaped hat like the Great Gazoo on *The Flintstones*. Suleiman was responsible for most of today's visible wall.

The Damascus Gate is the most ornate. An amazing piece of architecture. It's also the main entrance to the Muslim Quarter. Look up at the top and you'll see an inscription in Arabic. It translates something like *There is no God but Allah, and Muhammad is his messenger*. The gate is still there; Suleiman the Magnificent isn't. I hope I'm wrong, but something tells me he's not spending eternity on a lawn chair sipping a cold drink and cooling his desert-sandy toes in the River of Life.

Step outside the Zion Gate. The stones are riddled with bullet holes, a brutal reminder of the hard-fought Battle for Jerusalem in 1948. Yes, this is a city where blood has soaked into the streets.

The Dung Gate passes through the wall between the Jewish Quarter and the ancient City of David—and it's a busy place. It's the lowest of the gates, and in ancient times garbage was easier to move downhill—thus the name. Today, *despite* the name, the Dung Gate is one of the cleanest places in the city.

Close to the Dung Gate is Tanners' Gate. Excavated in the 1980s, restored in the 1990s, it's now in use as a pedestrian thoroughfare, helping ease traffic at the busy Dung.

In the 1880s, Christians living outside the northwestern wall made a ruckus for a gate that would give them direct access to the Christian Quarter. Ottoman Sultan Abdul Hamid II acquiesced, and the New Gate was formed—the highest gate in elevation in the city.

Herod's (or Flowers) Gate is an off-the-beaten-tourist-path entry accessing the Muslim Quarter in the north part of the city. The name is a little misleading since most scholars now believe Herod's palace was located across town to the south. If you're adventurous, Herod's Gate is a good place to get a local feel away from trinket and gift shops of the more tourist-traveled areas.

Around the corner to the east is Lions' Gate. Tour groups often pass through Lions' Gate to access the Church of Saint Anne, an amazing place. Legendary acoustics in the church make even a small group of singers sound like the Mormon Tabernacle Choir. A beautiful place to rest, pray, and listen.

So, as my Saudi friend had asked, "Where are the Christians?"

"They're there," I told her. "And more and more Israelis are coming to Christ all the time. But you have to look."

Christ Church in Jerusalem, the oldest Protestant church building in the Middle East, is one place to seek and find. And that's what several of us did one warm October day.

We'd spent the night at Masada and the morning down in the desert. We'd hiked En Gedi—the oasis where David hid out from King Saul—behind a field trip of laughing children guarded front and rear by men with automatic rifles. (Israelis take the protection of their children very seriously, kind of like Americans do their banks.) Afterward we'd pulled into a gas station in the West Bank, gassed up, bought frozen coffees, and joked with the guy who hawks camel rides to the tour buses.

Then up to Jerusalem. . . .

All of Jerusalem's ancient gates have their own, unique story, but if you want to *drive* into the Old City, the Jaffa Gate is your only ticket. I'd walked through many times but had never driven. The motor entrance is close to the old gate but separate. It took some serious map studying to figure it out. We headed into Jerusalem, an impressive convoy of two vans. I drove one while my friend, Ken, followed in the other. Christ Church also has a guesthouse, and we'd been lucky enough to book a few of the hard-to-get rooms. We'd be sleeping in the Old City for a few nights.

I'd called ahead. The manager told me security was tight, but she'd faxed our license plate numbers to the Jerusalem police. They'd be watching for us through a closed-circuit camera system and would open the gate remotely once they verified our plates. Didn't sound too complicated—and nothing ventured means nothing gained. Off we went.

Traffic getting into Jerusalem was bumper to bumper, and we were later than anticipated getting to the Jaffa entrance. I pulled up to the gate and, per our instructions, waited. Nothing happened. I waited some more. Maybe I'd misunderstood? I looked around for a button to push. A speaker, maybe. Nothing I could see. I'd just started dialing Christ Church on my phone when the barrier went up.

What do you know? I was in!

As the bar dropped behind me, I saw Ken pull up to repeat the process.

Christ Church wasn't hard to find. Only one right turn required. The big iron gate opened, and we drove in. A beautiful café and courtyard welcomed us. A place of immediate peace after the hectic drive.

My cell rang. It was Ken.

"They won't open the gate," he said.

"You're still there?"

"Yes."

I went into the guest house lobby and explained the situation to the girl at the desk. She rang the police, sparred for a while in Hebrew, then smiled. "It's taken care of."

My cell sounded again. "We're in," Ken said.

A few minutes later the second van joined ours. Everyone climbed out and stretched. We unloaded bags and assigned people rooms. I asked the desk girl where to park, and she pointed a long fingernail. "There's a parking lot back there. You can use it as long as you'd like."

I followed her point. An alley off the courtyard. Not much more than a crack in the ancient stone wall.

"I don't think we can fit. We're in vans," I said.

She smiled, shrugged, and went back to her work.

While our friends found their rooms, Ken and I walked over and took a look at the alley.

"What do you think?" I said.

"I think I understand what *camel through the eye of a needle* means a lot better now." (See Matthew 19:24.)

Nothing to it but to do it.

I went first. We flattened the mirrors down as far as we could. Ken guided from outside. Unbelievable. There couldn't have been more than an inch of clearance on either side of the van the whole way through. Somehow we both made it with our rented paint intact. We'd do the next couple days on foot, and I was glad I wouldn't have to execute our eye-of-the-needle exit for a while.

The next morning I was on the garden patio with a cup of coffee when my friend Steve approached.

"I was talking to the guy who runs the heritage museum here," he said. "He'd be happy to show us around and give us some history if we'd like. Can we fit it into our plans?"

My long-held theory about travel plans is that they're, at best, loose guidelines meant to be broken if something cool comes up. Hold everything with an easy grip because, especially in Israel, you never know what surprises might come your way.

"Yeah, man. Everything's flexible. Let's see what he has to say."

Roddey Brown turned out to be a great guy and a wealth of information. Jewish-American, his accent (deep South!) seemed a little out of place there among the old stones. We sat in the amazing, arched Ottoman-style church sanctuary while he told us the history. A lot of years, a lot of lives.

After visiting the sanctuary we walked the grounds. Archaeologists and scholars tell us Herod's palace occupied much of the Armenian Quarter. Jesus was taken there, to the Praetorium and to Pontius Pilate, to be tried and was consequently scourged. A powerful thing to be within yards of the spot such a pivotal moment in history took place.

"You want to see something fascinating?" Roddey said.

Of course we did.

We followed him into the coffee shop and then behind the counter. He ducked into a low passage and then down a steep flight of stairs. We found ourselves below the street in a stone room looking at the black mouth of a tunnel.

"Herodian," Roddey said. "They found it during original construction, but it was basically forgotten till the nineties. It goes way under the Old City. Maybe all the way to the Temple Mount."

I had to ask. "Can we go in?"

He smiled. "Of course not."

We spent the rest of the day wandering Jerusalem. It was late, quiet when we finally made it back to the Christ Church courtyard.

I noticed Roddey at a table in the little garden below our room. I sat down, and we talked about the day. I was curious about him. How had a Jew from the American South come to be working in a Christian church museum in Jerusalem?

"What brought you to Israel?" I asked.

"My mom was here, and she got sick. I came to take care of her. Plus, I thought Jerusalem would be a good place to party."

"But now you're here at Christ Church. Are you a Christian?"

"Absolutely. But I'd say I was atheist or, at best, agnostic when I first came to Israel."

"What changed?"

"I was invited to get together with a group of men, rabbis and others, to study, discuss, and debate. I came to realize the reality and truth of the Scriptures. I couldn't deny it. The next step was Yeshua. Was He—or was He not—the Messiah? I'm a skeptic. I struggled. But the facts were the facts. I couldn't deny the absolutely obvious truth Jesus is the Son of God. Now I'm here."

Roddey's story was unusual and wonderful. Outside of the tourists, Christianity is not the norm in Israel.

In fact, professing Christians only make up about 2 percent of Israel's population. Most are Catholic or Orthodox. Protestant and Messianic Jews don't quite reach 0.05 percent.

Remember my Saudi friend who asked, "Where are the Christians?" After all, Jesus was born in Bethlehem. Started His ministry in Galilee. Was crucified, buried, and resurrected very close to where Roddey and I sat drinking coffee beneath the darkening Jerusalem sky.

Is hers a complicated question? Maybe. Or maybe it's simple.

Many chalk the minuscule Christian population in Israel up to a continual clash of culture. Israel, the crossroads—conquered, razed, rebuilt, occupied . . . over and over and over again.

Some say the answer is political: the world is hostile to all things Jesus. After all, it was Christ Himself who told us, "You will be hated by all for My name's sake" (Luke 21:17).

Some blame the church itself. As one young Palestinian Christian told me, "The church in the West worships the Jews, not Jesus. We are forgotten."

Maybe all these points are valid. But maybe they're also only symptoms. Branches growing out of a single, spiritual root. Jesus said He came not to bring peace, but a sword. He told us the way was narrow and *few* would find it. And quoting the prophet Isaiah, the apostle Paul wrote that the gospel would be a stone of stumbling and a rock of offense.

But Jesus also promised victory. Victory over death, that ancient enemy. And a glorious peace in the age to come. (See Matthew 10:34; 7:13–14; Mark 10:34; Luke 18:33; Romans 9:33; and 1 Corinthians 15:54–55.)

So where are the Christians in Israel?

Roddey will tell you. . . .

They will come! When Yeshua returns *with His saints* to take His throne. When He rules the nations from His rightful place on the Temple Mount. They will come. . . .

And no stack of stones placed by human hands will keep Yeshua out. No tough words chiseled on a wall.

Keep an eye on the clouds.

The Christians will come.

CHAPTER 28

The Conversation

I believe The Conversation started when I was nine years old, the night before my first day of fifth grade.

That was the year my parents split, and all hell broke loose. At least as much hell as a nine-year-old can know. Which—come to think of it—is quite a bit. They went their separate ways, and I spun off into the cosmos.

I crash-landed in a back bedroom of my grandparents' house in California. I was angry. I was alone. I was scared. Autumn came. Fifth grade at an unfamiliar school populated with unfamiliar people. And I wasn't exactly the social type.

The little clock by the pullout-couch bed ticked. I'd been having nightmares, and I didn't want to sleep. So I stared at the ceiling. *Maybe I should pray.*

So I did.

Nothing. I just felt the same.

The clock ticked some more. I looked at the ceiling some more.

"Are You even out there?"

I could talk, but what I really needed to do was *hear*. To not be alone. Then an idea came to me. Maybe a nine-year-old-boy idea—or maybe not. Maybe an idea older than time, whispered on the wind—I don't know. Without really thinking I pulled a Bible off my grandfather's bookshelf, screwed my eyes shut, said a prayer, checked the wind, and stuck my finger on a page.

"For God has not given us a spirit of fear, but of power and of love and of a sound mind" (2 Timothy 1:7).

I read the words again.

Don't be afraid. . . .

I spoke into the darkness. "You're real?"

More real than anything you will ever know.

"I'm not alone?"

You've never been alone. And you never will be.

Yes, I believe The Conversation started when I was nine years old, the night before my first day of fifth grade. It hasn't always been an easy conversation. We've argued at times. Plenty of times. I've put my hands over my ears more often than I like to admit. But my Friend and I have walked together over a lot of peaks and through a lot of hard valleys. The road's been good—and the road's been hard. I've fought Him, and I've loved Him, and His hand has never left my shoulder.

I'm happy to report we don't fight much anymore.

And I'm even happier that our conversation will never end.

The journey goes on. . . .

Our ship pulled out of the Port of Piraeus, Greece, sky overcast, wind chilly. The boat was old and rusty; the crew, young and Russianish. Michelle and I took a tour of our stateroom. A very short tour. All it really involved was a single 360-degree turn. We agreed the place was cool in a 1960s Austin Powers floating-motor-home sort of way. A bell sounded through a speaker by the door. Then a woman's voice called all passengers outside for a safety drill. A few minutes later several hundred of us—resplendent in matching orange life vests—lined the worn, wooden decks getting our instructions should the old girl go into the drink. And, looking at her, the idea didn't seem too far-fetched.

So began our rusty, rocky Mediterranean cruise.

And I loved every single second of it.

There were a couple hundred people on the tour. Christian apologist and author Josh McDowell was the main speaking attraction, and yours truly signed on as tagalong troubadour. We had a great time sailing through the Greek islands. We toured John the Revelator's cave beneath an Orthodox church on Patmos and docked at the Crusader-built old city on Rhodes where Michelle and I spent the afternoon in a hidden courtyard café.

I did a concert in the ship's theater and afterward made a new friend of a Ukrainian balalaika player. Music was the only language we had in common, but we traded a few licks and got along fine.

One morning the ship pulled into Port Said, Egypt. Our group, escorted by several armed guards, climbed onto buses for a trip through Cairo and then on to Giza to see the pyramids. A huge man with a machine gun tucked under his suit coat boarded with us and took the front seat. Sammy, our local guide for the day, sat beside him. Michelle and I—bus captains—sat across the aisle from them, behind the driver.

The first thing I noticed as we flew down the freeway was that lane lines weren't much more than loose suggestions. We swerved everywhere there was a crack in the traffic as we—at seventy miles per hour—dodged camels, bicycles, and pedestrians—missing some of them by inches. Even our own buses fought and jockeyed for position. I had to scratch my head watching five forty-foot vehicles scrap like they were Formula One cars on the streets of Monte Carlo. Sammy held on tight, but our massive bodyguard hardly moved. I wondered if he was asleep.

"Hey, Sammy." I pointed out the window as one of our buses passed and cut us off, no more than six inches between our grill and his back bumper. "What's the deal? Aren't we all going to the same place?"

Sammy shrugged. "Welcome to Egypt. Don't try to understand it. We are who we are."

I noticed a few military vehicles—with manned guns mounted in the back—tracking alongside the buses. "Are they with us?"

"Yes," Sammy said. He offered no more comment.

Cairo traffic is nothing short of amazing. Cars weave, in all directions, surge and stop, and always with one long, continual horn blast. I looked down at a shining Mercedes-Benz next to a bailing-wire-and-duct-tape Datsun pickup with a full-grown Brahma bull standing in the back.

At one intersection our driver, for a reason I couldn't determine, decided it was time to make a U-turn. I watched the cars below scramble to get out of the way. One poor guy in a little sedan didn't have the room to retreat, and our right-rear tires went right over his hood. The bus dropped back to the pavement with a rocking thump. The man flew out of his car, screaming bloody murder.

Sammy said something in Arabic, and our bodyguard immediately stood and exited, face neutral. A serious wall of a man. I had a great view through the window as the machine gun came out from behind the suit coat and leveled.

This was not good.

In my heart, the old, familiar Conversation kicked into high gear.

"Jesus, You got this?"

From the foundations of the earth.

"This place is tense."

It's an old and long story.

I watched the guard say something to the offended driver who now looked like he might wet his pants. The man scrambled back into the sedan like a gopher into a hole. The machine gun went back into the suit coat, and our giant climbed back onto the bus, sat, and closed his eyes again.

"Hey, Sammy, what did he say to him?" I whispered.

Sammy queried in soft, rapid-fire Arabic. The big guard spoke without opening his eyes.

"He told him to get back in the car, or he would shoot him," Sammy said.

"You're not kidding?"

Sammy shrugged but didn't smile.

An old story.

We ate lunch on the Nile. We saw the pyramids. We visited the Museum of History.

A good day. A tourist day. But still, there was tension—an indefinable violence—in the air. *Spiritual,* I thought. Like heat. Or wind. Real enough. Something you could feel but couldn't see.

Night fell quickly as desert nights do. I was glad when we finally headed back toward the ship. Pedestrians dodged the headlights, ghosts in long robes and head coverings, as we flew back down the highway. Once I saw a form lying next to the concrete barrier in the median and felt a hard chill. A jolt all the way through my bones.

A body, I was sure. Hit and left there. A sack of bones on the side of the road in a land where life is cheap.

The big guard glanced over, and in the dim light of the bus, I caught his eyes, black and maybe a little sad.

Later, the ship's engines rumbled beneath us. The lights of Port Said rolled by in the porthole then disappeared.

An old story.

Conversation pressed.

I picked my guitar and wrote down some words:

Out of Egypt I have come
The devil barking at my heels . . .
Snapping at my wheels
Howling at the sun
Out of Egypt I have come
I'm wiping Cairo from my eyes
The breath of morning paints the sky . . .

A few short weeks after that bus ride, the Egyptian Revolution took place. We watched on the world news as the country flew into pieces.

I think about Sammy and the guard from time to time.

I wonder what happened to them.

Our ship docked again in Haifa, Israel. I found myself in Jerusalem, standing with my guitar at the bottom of the Southern Steps, the Temple Mount rising behind. A couple hundred people in front of me crowded onto that ancient stone. Jesus walked those stones. We worshipped then. As we should have.

Josh McDowell fist-bumped me as I finished and then stood to talk. Josh is an excellent fist-bumper. Birds flew in and out of a hole in the city wall. It's funny the little things we remember.

A woman approached me afterward to thank me for the worship time. "Isn't it amazing to worship here?" she said.

I looked down at the stone. Yes, it was special to be there. Surreal even.

But it was only stone—temporary. Not the eternal *realness* of Spirit.

She moved on, and I sat down on a step next to my guitar case. I put my hand on the stone, worn smooth and cool to the touch.

And in an instant I was nine again, listening to the clock tick my whispered prayers into the dark.

More real than anything you will ever know.

You will never, ever be alone.

I thought about Egypt and Rhodes. About a barroom I knew in Hollywood. I thought about my home in Idaho. And, for some reason, about a windy, midnight stop for gas in Crow, Montana. Most of all, I thought about the impossibly long, one-block walk to school on the first day of fifth grade and the arm I felt around my shoulders every step of the way.

I'd felt that arm in Egypt too.

I felt it there on the Southern Steps.

The Conversation started when I was nine years old, the night before my first day of fifth grade.

On it goes.

CHAPTER 29

The Climb

I love America. I really do.

But the scenery along the American Dream highway has changed over the years. Not nearly as many two-bedroom ranchers and white picket fences. Strip malls soak up the acreage instead. And we all must have been watching Netflix when some pack of hair-sprayed hucksters stole Billy Graham's microphone and 50 Cent knocked off Duke Ellington in a drive-by. We lost Cash and gained Bieber. Traded Hitchcock and John Wayne for CGI robots. I'm fairly sure Ronald Reagan never took a selfie in the mirror or posted pictures of his sushi, but—love him or hate him—you can't say the same about the current leader of the free world.

Rise and shine, campers! It's a brand-new day.

We wear a lot of costumes—suits and ties, boots and Wranglers, tie-dye, flannel, skinny jeans, burkas. . . . We are worshippers at every turn, though worshipping the One to whom we owe our breath falls in and out of vogue. We argue a lot. We give each other the finger and shoot spit wads across the political aisle. We shout our theology with our hands over our ears.

We are rich, increased in goods, in need of nothing, yet will be satisfied with no less than *more*.

But, just like our parents in the garden, when the chips are down, we somehow remember who we are. When things really get tough, we turn off the television and put down our *Self* magazines. We blink sleep out of our eyes. In those moments we are humbled. We relax our fists. Petulance ebbs, and we are—once again—broken children reaching for the arms of our Father.

For a moment, we are America again.

And He holds us.

And in His arms we are great . . . because He is great.

Then the noise comes back.

One consistent thing about our country is, through good times and bad, the American dream rolls on. All are welcome. It's a grand highway, wide and comfortable. LA to NYC, Fargo to Laredo, and all points in between. No matter who you are, you can look at the world's biggest ball of string while you gas up, and there's always free coffee at Wall Drug.

In America the future is something we take for granted.

Not so, Israel. From an earthly perspective, Israel's future is about as solid as morning mist.

Some years ago in the Istanbul airport, I found myself the lone American stuck in the middle of a cattle-herd press of bodies boarding a plane for Tel Aviv. In the east, the concept of waiting in line gets fuzzy, and things come down to the survival of the fittest. We all had assigned seats, so this made no sense to me. But, hey, I wasn't in Kansas—or Idaho—anymore. The Israelis around me took it all in stride and settled in. Nothing new to them. Israelis scrap on a daily basis. They live life with an urgency that comes from thousands of years of not being guaranteed another five minutes on the planet. With the world's history of anti-Semitism—so unreasonable it can only be spiritual—their very existence is nothing short of miraculous. Bottom line? Take God out of the equation, and there's no way Israel still exists.

After landing in Tel Aviv, I connected with a handful of other American dreamers for a countrywide excursion. On a warm afternoon a few days later, we were headed up into the Golan Heights when I saw several police cars, lights flashing, up ahead. I slowed our van as we approached. At least a hundred bicyclists were just hitting a steep, winding grade ahead of the officers. The police cars were traffic control. We were apparently the traffic.

The police cars weren't moving over, making it clear we'd get to the top along with the slowest pedaler. We rolled the windows down and let in the nice breeze. Might as well get comfortable. I didn't mind much. I had good company, it was a beautiful day, and the scenery was nice. The hills, October brown, were dotted with olive trees. The narrow two-lane road wound upward. My friends loved to sing, and they did.

A rusty barbed-wire fence crept up on our left paralleling the road. A faded yellow sign with a red triangle said DANGER—MINES in English, Hebrew, and Arabic. On the other side of the fence, a little boy and an old man watched over a flock of sleepy sheep. The old man raised a gnarled hand as we passed. I waved back, wondering how in the world a person herded sheep in the middle of an old minefield. I thought about that pair for a long time as we crept along. *What home waited for them at the end of the day? What did they hope for? What did they dream about? What was it like for a little boy to fall asleep every night to the distant rumble of bombs?*

We moved on. Forty-five minutes . . . an hour . . . maybe more. My friends ran low on songs. I think we all might have run low on patience. Finally, at the top of the hill, the cyclists turned off, and the police cars let us pass.

We forgot the cyclists and spent a long day exploring as the sun moved in a slow arc overhead. By late afternoon we'd had enough heat, and we drove back down the way we'd come. I looked for the boy and the old man, but they were gone. Buildings became more frequent, then a town. My friends saw an ice cream place and asked to stop. Ice cream and Israel go hand in hand. A little something against the heat of the afternoon.

I turned up a side road and into a parking lot. They headed into the ice cream joint, but I spotted a coffee shop at the far end of the little mall. Good, I needed something to help keep my eyes open on the drive south. The place was air-conditioned and packed with— you guessed it—cyclists. I waited, milling around with the group bunched in front of the counter and hoping to catch someone's attention. When I finally did, the counter girl understood the word *Americano* well enough. The machine hissed steam, and she handed me a cup. Hot black happiness.

Through the window I could see my friends hadn't come out of the ice cream place, so I looked around for somewhere to sit. I found an empty chair across a table from one of the cyclists. A middle-aged guy. Salty dried sweat crusted his face and jersey. I sat and offered him a *shalom*. He was slumped low in his chair, tiny espresso next to his water bottle on the table in front of him. Clearly, it had been a long ride. Even though he was obviously exhausted, he still had that tough-as-nails, shaved-head IDF look that said he knew sixty-three different ways to kill a person with his shoestring. For a few seconds I thought he'd ignore me.

"*Shalom*," his voice all sun, tanks, and gravel.

"Were you with that big group of bikes out on Highway 99?" I said.

He sipped his coffee. I thought he might not have understood me, but then he met my eye. His English turned out to be excellent. "Yes, a fifty-kilometer ride."

"A long way."

He shrugged and sipped again. Not a warm, fuzzy guy, but at least I felt tolerated. He hadn't killed me, and the coffee was good. Ahead of the game, if you ask me.

I pointed to his jersey and tried again. "I was in a van today behind you guys."

His look said, *Too bad for you.*

I realized he might have thought I was complaining. I told him I wasn't, that it had been a nice drive. For some reason I thought about mentioning the old man and the boy in the minefield, but I didn't.

"Tough climb on a bike," I said instead.

He drained his cup and stood. "This is Israel. Everything is a tough climb." He walked off, bike shoes clacking on the tiled floor. No goodbye *shalom*. He hadn't offered a handshake. I hadn't expected one.

I watched my companions come out of the ice cream shop and sit down at a shaded table. I knew I should go join them, but I didn't right away. Heat waves danced on the hills. The AC felt good. My coffee-drinking cyclist passed the window and gave me a chin-jut *adios*. I can't say I'd made a friend, but I'd kind of come to admire the guy. He exemplified the dogged strength of these people, this nation. Babylon to Auschwitz to Isis, the Jews have done more than survive. They have fought. And they have lived. They might not feel they are guaranteed another five minutes, but if they get them, they're going to wring every ounce of life out of them. Joy, pain, and everything in between. They'll get on their bikes and conquer the hill. Along the way they'll pass no rest stops or big balls of twine. No Wall Drug Store.

And, at the end of the ride, they'll pay for their coffee.

CHAPTER 30

Looking for the Porch Light

A bankrupt sun limped down into the Negev like a tired old man. My headlights reeled in the highway.

Words from a long time ago:

I got nothing but time and a broken white line
Cigarette burns on the dashboard . . .

Another desert. Another life.

There's always been something for me in the desert at night. I can't explain it. Lord knows, I've tried. A thousand songs prove it— most of them in the trash, a few rolled up in a reel of tape somewhere, others still bouncing through the ether. Even as a child, lying on the seat of my dad's truck, watching stars track our gravel-road progress, I felt it. A voice, a whisper, a fleeting *something*. Out past the dashboard lights and Hank Williams's AM-radio purple sky. Something ancient. Deep and perfect. And it knew my name.

My headlights caught two yellow eyes just far enough off the road that I couldn't make out their owner. *Probably a jackal* . . . like the coyotes back home.

In my mind, the Negev and the Mojave are brothers of sorts. Even the asphalt rushing under my wheels felt familiar. A new road for me, but one I'd driven a thousand times between Yuma and Phoenix. Or Tucson and Las Cruces, New Mexico.

I rolled down the window. The air warm. Full of dead campfires, Merle Haggard, and cheap whiskey. Clouds of glory rolling down canal banks, Mexico across the river.

Past and present blurred a little.

I hear mariachi static on the radio

And the tubes, they glow in the dark. . . .

Sure, this was the Negev, not Yuma. But the same Voice, warm and familiar, spoke to me from the night.

My fellow travelers were asleep. Fine with me. I was comfortable out there in the empty with my Friend. I drove while He called the dance for those million times a million vibrating stars.

A few hours to go.

Time to go home. On the other side of the world a porch light burned, waiting for me. And I was ready to be there.

Red taillights up ahead. A car moving slowly. At least slower than I was. I blew by, window cracked, desert air soft on my face. In my rearview mirror headlights grew as the car I'd just passed caught up. I knew he would. I had to smile as he passed me and resumed his original speed. A consistent Israeli driving habit I'm still trying to comprehend.

I passed him again.

He passed me again.

We crossed swords for a while. Nothing personal. The way of the world.

One time over dinner I asked an Israeli friend why his countrymen did this—the pass and re-pass thing. He just chuckled. "I suppose we don't want you to get there first."

"Where is *there?*"

A frown and shrug. "Wherever."

Our van wound down into a canyon. The air cooled a few degrees. Flat and straight for a while, then we climbed. I knew where we were now. In a few minutes we'd top out into the wasteland town of Mitzpe Ramon. Out to our left, the largest erosion crater in the world stretched into the black. The Ramon Crater—tonight nothing but a massive, sandy basket of starlight.

A couple days ago we'd stood out on the rim of that expanse. I'd watched a young couple from the Black Hebrew community there play with their small children. The wind had whipped the woman's colorful African dress. The man helped her hold it down while the kids laughed and chased each other.

The town was quiet and dark as we drove through. The Black Hebrews, tired from their 1960s exodus out of the Chicago race wars, were long asleep. Of course they were tired. They'd carried their art and jazz and heavenly visions a long, long way. We drove on, leaving them to slumber on that windswept cliff while the ghosts of Whitney Houston and Mahalia Jackson hummed plainsong in blue harmony.

A couple hours to go.

More dark. More stars.

Finally, the horizon began to glow and lighten. A bit later the outskirts of Tel Aviv loomed. I pulled the van into a truck stop to diesel it up before returning it to the rental company. My friends woke and rolled out for restrooms and food.

The truck stop doubled as a restaurant. It was busy. By the sound and look and laughter, I guessed this was the after-closing-time crowd. One clerk served the whole place, trying his sweaty best to ring up self-serve meals along with the gas. This meant a thirty-minute wait while he worked his way through all the people with all their needs. Outside, cars and trucks were stacked ten deep at every pump.

Honking horns and wheels moaning from the highway. The wind warm off the desert. A paper cup bounced across the asphalt as we pulled back onto the road. Sand, fields, industrial buildings. As we pressed closer to the city, minarets glowed green on the horizon.

We made quick time getting into Ben Gurion. Only a car or two in each line. Security heavy as always. Machine-gun-wielding soldiers stacked two deep at every kiosk: the looks on their faces said they meant business. But only a brief verbal exchange, and we were through.

We unloaded as the rental attendant gave our van the once-over. I felt a little sad saying goodbye to that dented old Citroën. It smelled like cigarettes and old socks, but it'd been a faithful Little Train That Could over mountain and valley, through desert and oasis, for the better part of two weeks. Charioted us in style through lands of prophets and gods.

But there were planes to catch.

I hugged my friends goodbye. They handed me a postcard—Photoshopped Elvis in a prayer shawl at the Western Wall. I watched as they disappeared through security. Good and adventurous traveling companions.

I had over twenty-four hours till my own flight. No more van. No hotel booked. I weighed options, then put down the scale, and went to the sandwich shop. I don't remember the name of the place, but they have the best eggplant sandwiches anywhere. Actually, they have the only eggplant sandwich I've ever even heard of, but *so* good.

Sandwich and coffee in hand, I found a vacant plastic chair and supped like a displaced king.

I checked my watch. Only twenty-three hours and forty minutes to go.

I weighed options again. The smart move would be to go hunt down a hotel room and get some sleep. Then again, nothing is cheap in Tel Aviv. I'd be out a hundred and fifty bucks at least. Plus the taxi. And, frankly, I was hotel-ed out. Besides, I had a long plane ride ahead. Plenty of sleep time there.

No problem. I had ready food available and a good book in my pack. I'd find a padded chair or bench somewhere and spend a long, blissful day doing nothing.

Except—as I quickly discovered—there isn't one padded *anything* at Ben Gurion Airport. Why hadn't I ever noticed that before? Like much of Israel, it's a place built for efficiency, not comfort. Hard chairs, hard benches, hard floors.

I started with the chair. When the print blurred, I finally admitted to myself I was exhausted. I found an out-of-the-way-looking spot on the floor and stretched out.

I once slept on a bed made of adobe (no joke) in Central America. I would have taken it in a heartbeat.

I talked to my Friend. "If I remember right, You had a stone for a pillow. So this isn't so bad, right?"

"*If you say so.*"

"I could get a hotel."

"*You could.*"

"It's expensive. And far away. I'd have to get a taxi too."

"*I own the cattle on a thousand hills.*"

"They take shekels, not cows."

"*Your call.*"

A half world away my wife slept in our comfortable bed. I missed them both.

I must have dozed. A boot woke me, and I cracked an eye at it. Not a friendly boot. A big, black steel-toed job. Stuck solidly on the foot of a well-armed security officer.

I sat up.

He said something in Hebrew. Definitely not the smiley type.

I shook my head. "I'm American. Sorry, I don't speak Hebrew."

"What are you doing?"

A few smart-aleck replies leapt to mind, but it's a good rule of thumb not to verbally mess with jackbooted Israeli security guys. I didn't want to have any backroom conversations under a dim light bulb. "Sleeping."

"You are with a group?"

"No. I'm alone. Waiting for my flight."

"Stand up."

I did.

He held out a hand. "Let me see your ticket and passport, please."

I stood and fished my reservation from my pack. He took it and looked it over.

"Your flight is not until tomorrow?"

"Yes."

"You're waiting here?"

"Yes."

"Why?"

"Because hotels are expensive."

He looked at the paper again and then gave an Israeli shrug. "Sweet dreams."

Another eggplant sandwich, then a tuna, several cups of coffee, and a couple novels later, I made it through security and onto a Turkish Airlines flight bound for Istanbul and points beyond. I'm telling you, padding never felt so good. I lay my head against the glass as the acceleration of takeoff pressed me back into the seat. The horizon tipped. Tel Aviv sprawled beneath me. A wisp of cloud between us now. I managed to pick out the white and blue of the Royal Beach Hotel and the American Embassy next door. Propelled forward by a thin wake of white, a fishing boat chugged out of the old Jaffa Port. The country would go on about its business without me.

Goodbye, Israel.

I will be back. In this life or the next.

One day earthly home will burst into heavenly home, black and white into living color.

The coastline blended into the clouds and then faded altogether. Only the Mediterranean, deep blue, beneath us now. The window cool against my forehead. My eyes heavy. My Friend's embrace warm. We'd had adventures, He and I. We'd seen some things. We'd see some more.

For now, my own earthly place beckoned, and I couldn't wait to be there. Still, it's never easy to go home. I would miss these people.

I knew my friends would smile and ask, "What was it like? Did you see the Wailing Wall? How about the Garden Tomb? Was it amazing?"

Yes, I would say, it *was* amazing. That's what I always say when I return from Israel. And it's true—every trip unique, every trip special, every trip *Israel*. I'd tell them about an aging soldier and a cold rain. About a miniature SpongeBob grifter on the Ramparts Walk. About a crusty motel owner. About an African girl and a curly haired dog.

I'd tell them about angels and blood and miracles. And a heavenly love so deep and precious it hurt.

"Oh . . . ," they'd say, confused. "But did you get to walk where Jesus walked?"

Then I'd think about my Friend and our path. The feel of His robe in my hand and the way my traveling shoes fit perfectly into His footprints.

Oh yes, I'd tell them, I *definitely* walked where Jesus walked.

Acknowledgments

Jesus has been my constant and good companion for as long as I can remember—a compass without which I would be lost.

Without the prodding of my literary agent, Jim Hart, this book would have happily napped on a pool float in the backwater of my brain. Thanks for popping the raft, Jim. You made this thing swim.

Michelle, my traveling partner these many years, I love you. Hang on to those coffee punch-cards—we have a million more miles ahead.

Ransom, Sarah, Willow, and almost Rob (welcome to the family, man!). As is our custom, my daughter Willow patiently let me read the first draft out loud to her. I'm happy to report she laughed and cried in all the right parts.

Mom, the road has had its dark parts and the game hasn't always been fair. But with losing hand or royal flush, you always trusted the Dealer. Thanks for your example.

Kyle Olund, Leeanna Nelson, Nicole Pavlas, and all the Worthy family—thanks for taking a chance on this little book. Your enthusiasm encourages me more than you know.

Bill and Susie Perkins and Compass International graciously took us on our first trip to Israel. What a blessing it was and continues to be. Thank you, guys!

The people whose company and conversations have shaped my stories are far too many to name, but here are a few: Ben Ortize, Dan Stolebarger, Ted and Linda Walker, Michael Paul, Randall Murphree, Tod Hornby, Ronny Simon, John Higgins, Randy and Leslie Stonehill, Bob Bennet, Phil Keaggy, Ray Ware, Paul Clark, Chik Chikeles—and so many other pastors, friends, and wisdom givers who have loved us, lifted us, and lit our path.

Finally, to all you other backroads seekers out there—strength on the journey, my friends. Keep your eyes on the Bright Morning Star. We'll see you down the trail.

Shalom,

Buck

About the Author

BUCK STORM grew up in Yuma, Arizona—a true son of the American Southwest. He is a critically acclaimed touring singer/songwriter and the author of two novels—*Truck Stop Jesus* and the Selah Award finalist *The Miracle Man*. His short story, "A Waffle Stop Story of Love and Pistols" was featured in *21 Days of Grace: Stories That Celebrate God's Unconditional Love*. Whether lyrics or prose, Buck writes about this mixed-up, out-of-control, beautiful cacophony we call humanity—about life as he sees it and sometimes just how he'd like it to be. Buck and his wife, Michelle, have a happy love story, a hideout in Hayden, Idaho, and two wonderful, grown children.

For more of Buck Storm's music, books,
or to inquire about future Israel trips, please visit:

www.buckstorm.com

IF YOU ENJOYED THIS BOOK, WILL YOU CONSIDER SHARING THE MESSAGE WITH OTHERS?

Mention the book in a blog post or through Facebook, Twitter, or upload a picture through Instagram.

Recommend this book to those in your small group, book club, workplace, and classes.

Head over to facebook.com/buckstormauthor/, "LIKE" the page, and post a comment as to what you enjoyed the most.

Tweet "I recommend reading #FindingJesusInIsrael by @BuckStormMusic // @worthypub"

Pick up a copy for someone you know who would be challenged and encouraged by this message.

Write a book review online.

WORTHY®
PUBLISHING

Visit us at worthypublishing.com

twitter.com/worthypub

instagram.com/worthypub

facebook.com/worthypublishing

youtube.com/worthypublishing